Sitana: A Mountain Campaign on the Borders of Afghanistan in 1863

A. Original position of the British force in the Umbeylah Pass.
B. Eagle's Nest picket.   C. Crag picket.
C. D. Front of Chamberlain's second position, 18th Novr
E. Scene of General Garvock's victory, 15th Decr
L. Laloo.   U. Umbeylah.   K. Koorfa.   H. Bonair.

THE UMBEYLAH PASS AND CHUMLA VALLEY

Sitana: A Mountain Campaign on the Borders of Afghanistan in 1863

The British Raj and Tribesmen on the Northwestern Frontier of India

John Adye

LEONAUR

Sitana: A Mountain Campaign on the Borders of Afghanistan in 1863
The British Raj and Tribesmen
on the Northwestern Frontier of India
by John Adye

First published under the title
Sitana: A Mountain Campaign on the Borders of Afghanistan in 1863

Leonaur is an imprint of Oakpast Ltd

Copyright in this form © 2011 Oakpast Ltd

ISBN: 978-0-85706-639-8 (hardcover)
ISBN: 978-0-85706-640-4 (softcover)

http://www.leonaur.com

Publisher's Notes

Contents

Preface

In the autumn of 1863, the British Government sent an expedition of 5,000 men into the mountains beyond the Northwest Frontier of India, and on the confines of Afghanistan. The object was to punish certain Fanatics and independent tribes, who had for a long time been committing depredations in our border districts. The march of our columns into the mountains so excited the anger of the neighbouring Mahomedan tribes, that a general combination ensued against us, and the force had to fight hard to maintain its ground, and to accomplish its purpose.

Having been present towards the close of the operations, I am in hopes that my knowledge of the scene will have enabled me to give a clear account of the campaign, which, though short, was a very interesting one, both in its military and political aspects, and more especially as having occurred in a part of the country never before entered by British troops.

In drawing up my account, I have consulted the following works:—

1. Report on the Settlement of the Peshawur District; by the late Major Hugh James, C. B., Commissioner.

2. Report showing the Relations of the British Government with the Tribes on the North-west Frontier; by Mr. Temple, former Secretary of the Punjab.

3. Papers relating to the Disturbances in the North-west Frontier of India. Presented to Parliament, 1864.

4. Military Despatches of the operations.

5. Treaties with the Frontier Tribes. Aitchison, 1864.

I have also been favoured with a copy of the Minute of Sir William Denison, who on the death of Lord Elgin succeeded as Viceroy of India at a critical period of the campaign.

John Adye,

Colonel Royal Artillery.

London, Nov. 1866.

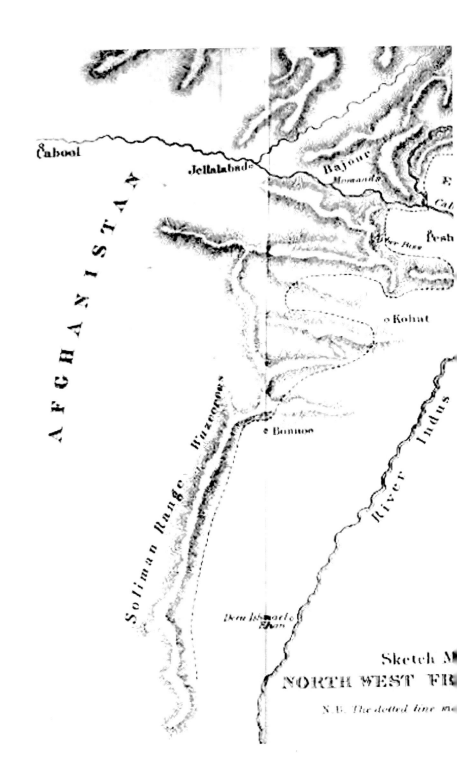

Sketch M
NORTH WEST FR
N.B. The dotted line m

Map of the
...NTIER OF INDIA.
...kn the British Frontier.

CHAPTER 1

The Scene of the War

About forty miles above the old fort of Attock, on the Indus, and just beyond the north-west frontier of our territories in India, stands a mountain called the Mahabun. Late in the autumn of 1863, this mountain was the scene of a short but severe campaign, between the English and their Afghan neighbours, and which at one time assumed the larger dimensions of a frontier war. The scene is distant, and little known to most people at home; and as the war, which lasted two months, was at an end almost before intelligence of it could reach England, no great or general interest was ever felt in the subject, and it is already perhaps almost forgotten. Still, in many respects, this little campaign was a very interesting one. Mountain warfare so greatly enhances the ordinary difficulties of moving troops and of modern fighting, that in a purely military point of view such an operation is an interesting study.

Politically, also, our dealings with those fierce races who fringe, as it were, our Indian Empire, and who are the advance-guards of Central Asia, deserve careful thought. And when we consider that, in the battles on the Mahabun, thirty-six English officers, and between eight and nine hundred men, were killed or wounded, it would seem that some account of the varied incidents, and of the stern combats which took place on the slopes of that far-distant mountain, may prove of interest even to those who usually hardly care to study the dry details of military or political matters.

A glance at the map will show that the frontier of that part of India of which we are now speaking consists for the most part of mountain-chains, the valley of Peshawur, which lies in the extreme corner, being in great measure encircled by them. On its northern side, the scene of the present war, steep and rugged spurs, radiating from the lofty heights of the Hindoo Koosh, and enclosing sheltered valleys of varied size, form a rather uncertain and irregular boundary. The whole of these mountains, extending for several hundred miles along our border, are inhabited by tribes who, although in great measure independent, still bear a close affinity to the Afghan nation immediately behind them: and it is further to be observed, that even in the plains within our own jurisdiction on the frontier, the people generally, as regards race, nationality, and religion, have many points of resemblance with the mountaineers; so that, although the geographical features of the country are strongly marked, there is no such sharp distinction between the inhabitants on either side.

During the last twenty years, which is the duration of our rule in the Punjab, we have been engaged in a series of desultory campaigns with these tribes over the border, the last and most considerable being that to be related. Before entering into its details, it may be interesting to consider shortly the characteristics of the tribes, and the policy hitherto pursued by us towards them, and this will be readily done by a few extracts from the reports of our frontier authorities.

The late Major James, when Commissioner of Peshawur, wrote [1] of them as follows:—

Those who have travelled much amongst the Afghans, and visited them in their sequestered valleys, retain a pleasing impression of the general characteristics of their homes. Emerging from wild and craggy defiles, with a solitary tower here and there, perched up on the overhanging rocks, the stranger comes suddenly upon the village site; springs of refreshing clearness pass from rocky cisterns to

1. Report on the Settlement of the Peshawur District, by Major Hugh R. James, C.B.

the brook which had repeatedly crossed his path in the defile, and which is here fringed with rows of weeping-willow and edged with brightest sward. The village is half hid from view with overshadowing mulberry and poplar trees, the surrounding fields enamelled with a profusion of wild flowers, and fragrant with aromatic herbs At some distance is seen a wood of thorn and tamarisk, in which are the graves of the village forefathers; an enclosing wall of stone and the votive shreds, which are suspended from the overhanging tree, pointing out the *zizarut* of some saintly ancient, which children pass with awe, and old men with reverence.

The dream of peace and comfort which the contempla-tion of such scenes suggests is, however, rudely dispelled by the armed ploughman, who follows his cattle with a matchlock slung at his back; by the watchtower, occupied by a party of men to guard the growing crops; and by the heaps of stones visible in all directions, each of which marks the spot of some deed of blood. We cease, indeed, to be surprised at the love of home which is so marked a feature of the Afghan character, for, reared in a little world of his own, the associations of his childhood must make a more than ordinary impression on his mind; but we might expect that such spots would engender other feelings than those which lurk in the breast of the robber and assassin.

Mr. Temple, the former secretary to the Lieutenant-Governor of the Punjab, writing a few years ago, speaks on the whole very unfavourably of our frontier neighbours. He says:—[2]

Now these tribes are savages, noble savages perhaps, and not without some tincture of virtue and generosity, but still absolutely barbarians nevertheless. They have for the most part no education. They have nominally a religion, but Mahomedanism, as understood by them, is no better, or perhaps is actually worse, than the creeds of the wildest

---

2. Selections from the Records of the Government of India.

races on earth. In their eyes the one great commandment is blood for blood, and fire and sword for all *infidels*, that is for all people not Mahomedans.

They are superstitious and priest-ridden. But the priests (*moollas*) are as ignorant as they are bigoted, and use their influence simply for preaching crusades against unbelievers, and inculcate the doctrine of rapine and bloodshed against the defenceless people of the plain. The hill-men are sensitive in regard to their women, but their customs in regard to marriage and betrothal are very prejudicial to social advancement. At the same time they are a sensual race. They are very avaricious: for gold they will do almost anything except betray a guest. They are thievish and predatory to the last degree; the Pathan mother often prays that her son may be a successful robber. They are utterly faithless to public engagements; it would never occur to their minds that an oath on the *Koran* was binding if against their interests.

It must be added that they are fierce and bloodthirsty. They are never without weapons: when grazing their cattle, when driving beasts of burden, when tilling the soil, they are still armed. They are perpetually at war with each other. Every tribe and section of a tribe has its internecine wars, every family its hereditary blood-feuds, and every individual his personal foes. There is hardly a man whose hands are unstained. Each person counts up his murders; each tribe has a debtor and creditor account with its neighbours, life for life. Reckless of the lives of others, they are not sparing of their own. They consider retaliation and revenge to be the strongest of all obligations. They possess gallantry and courage themselves, and admire such qualities in others.

Men of the same party will stand by one another in danger. To their minds hospitality is the first of duties. Any person who can make his way into their dwellings will not only be safe, but will be kindly received; but as soon as he has left the roof of his entertainer, he may be robbed or killed. They are charitable to the indigent of their own tribe. They possess the pride of birth, and regard ancestral associations. They are not averse to civilisation whenever they have felt its benefits; they are fond of trading, and also of cultivating; but they are too fickle and excitable to be industrious in agriculture, or anything else. They will take military service, and, though impatient of discipline, will prove faithful unless excited by fanaticism. Such briefly is their character, replete with the unaccountable inconsistencies, with that mixture of opposite vices and virtues belonging to savages.

In speaking of the conduct of these tribes and of our policy towards them, Mr. Temple continues as follows:—

Such being their character, what has been their conduct towards us? They have kept up old quarrels or picked new ones with our subjects in the plains or valleys near the frontier; they have descended from the hills, and fought their battles out in our own territory. They have plundered and burnt our villages, and slain our subjects. They have committed minor robberies and isolated murders without number; they have often levied black-mail from our villages; they have intrigued with the disaffected everywhere, and tempted our loyal subjects to rebel; and they have for ages regarded the plain as their preserves, and its inhabitants as their game.

When inclined for cruel sport, they sally forth to rob and murder, and occasionally to take prisoners into captivity for ransom. They have fired upon our troops, and even killed our own officers in our own territories. They give an asylum to every malcontent or proclaimed criminal who can escape from British justice. They traverse at will our territories, enter our villages, trade in our markets; but few British subjects, and no servant of the British Government, would dare to enter their country on any account whatever.

In return for this, what has been the conduct of the British Government towards them? It has recognised their independence—it has asserted no jurisdiction in regard to them; it has claimed no revenue from them, and no tribute except in one case, and that as a punishment. But it has confirmed whatever fiefs they held within its territory; it has uniformly declared that it seeks no fiscal or territorial aggrandisement, and that it only wants, and is resolved to have, tranquillity on the frontier. It has never extended its jurisdiction one yard beyond the old limits of the Sikh dominions. Nothing has been annexed that was not a portion of the Punjab as we found it. Whatever revenue has been paid to the British Government was equally paid to its predecessors, only at a higher rate.

In one solitary instance has it accepted tribute in satisfaction for offences: in all other cases of misconduct it has avoided making any pecuniary demand in its own behalf. It has claimed no feudal or political ascendancy over the independent hill-tribes; it has abstained from any interference in, or connection with, their affairs; it has taken no part in their contests, and has never assisted either party; it has striven to prevent its own subjects from entering into disputes with them. . . . . . But when kindness, conciliation, and confidence all fail; when outrages, from their serious character, or from their constant repetition, exceed the bounds of toleration; when the blood of our subjects cries from the ground; when our territory has been invaded, and our sovereign rights flagrantly violated, and all this in the utter absence of provocation: then we either make reprisals from, or lay an embargo upon, or use military force against, the offending tribe or section of tribe.

The above account may be taken as a rough sketch of the hardy people on the frontier, but is far too harsh and sweeping in its general conclusions. As the predominant power in India, we are very apt thus arbitrarily to condemn the character, conduct, and policy of the Eastern races with whom we are brought into contact. We constitute ourselves the judges of our own quarrels, and measure too rigidly, by an European standard, men who have been brought up under far different conditions of life. It is very possible that in the majority of quarrels we may be more absolutely in the right than our adversaries, and may be able to argue our case more skilfully than they; but if we do so in a high-handed domineering spirit, arising from consciousness of superior power, we are sure to be met by their hearty hatred and by an appeal to arms.

As regards these frontier people, we should remember that they are the vanguard, as it were, of those nations of Central Asia who, from time immemorial, have sent forth a succession of conquerors over the plains of India. Until our arrival in the East, the various Mahomedan kingdoms were created by invading armies from the North-west, so that the vast plains which now constitute our empire have hitherto been looked upon as the invariable field for Afghan enterprise. Within the last century, however, these nations of Central Asia have beheld dynasty after dynasty upset by us in turn; they have seen the tide of English conquest steadily advancing, until at length we are standing face to face with them, and our standards are flying over the forts at the very foot of their mountains.

Under these circumstances it can, perhaps, scarcely be a matter of wonder that our acts should be looked upon with suspicion, if not with hatred, and that our neighbours should doubt the professed policy of non-intervention and peace. Our advance has hitherto been steadily onwards to the North-west; and if geographical difficulties, and a bare inhospitable region, now seem to check it for a time, it is not surprising that those who live in the mountain fastnesses beyond the border should believe that their safety depends more upon their own bravery than upon our forbearance. These hungry mountaineers, whose ordinary life is that of armed shepherds on the bare hillside, or who gain a precarious livelihood from the cultivation of scanty crops in the secluded valleys, looking down on the shining fertile plains and prosperous villages far below them, almost intuitively feel a longing to resume the traditional habits of their enterprising forefathers.

The temptation is even greater than of yore, though the means of gratification are far more perilous. It does not follow that they must needs be mere faithless savages because they view us with suspicion, nor can it be expected that the hereditary instincts of centuries can be overcome in a day. These border races are, physically, very handsome; they are brave, courteous, and hospitable. They are devotedly attached to their country, their women, and their religion; and although, from traditional policy and old habits, they are likely to prove troublesome neighbours, our relations with them can hardly be friendly, if we fail to appreciate in them those manly virtues which amongst ourselves are deemed worthy of all admiration. In the very war which we are now about to consider, it will be found that many of these men, from either side of the border, fought as soldiers under our flag, and exhibited a bravery and faithful devotion scarcely to be surpassed even by our own countrymen.

CHAPTER 2

The Punjab Irregular Force

The late East India Company, during the continuance of their government, fostered many anomalies in their cumbrous military system, and constantly violated many of the recognised rules of army procedure; but, perhaps, in no case did they do so more palpably and unaccountably than in their creation of numerous local forces, commanded by English officers, but removed entirely from the authority of the commander-in-chief. These contingents—composed of the three arms, and provided with siege-trains, arsenals, and reserves—in some cases assumed the dimensions of small armies. They were scattered all over the country, and thus often enabled the civil power to carry out coercive semi-military proceedings, without having their operations submitted to public view, or to the control and possible criticism of superior military authority. The great majority of these dangerous contingents happily disappeared in the general convulsion of 1857, but a few still remain, relics of a bygone system.

Perhaps the most celebrated of these local independent armies still existing, is that called the Punjab Irregular Force. It is just, however, at once to state, that although it may be open to criticism, as being removed from the control of the highest military authority, as a fighting body its deeds have ever shown it to be thoroughly well-manned and admirably led. This force appears to have been originally raised in 1849. It now consists of six field and mountain batteries, and of five cavalry and twelve infantry regiments, the whole amounting to upwards of 10,000 men. It is composed entirely of native troops, and is recruited on the frontier, and from the very Pathan races of whom an account has just been given. The great majority of men in the ranks are from the districts within the border, though there are also many from the neighbouring mountains, the one set of men being hardly distinguishable from the other.

The regiments and batteries of the Punjab Force are thinly distributed, at various isolated stations, for hundreds of miles along the north-west frontier, and are provided with means of conveyance and accessories, so as to be ready for immediate movement. The officers are carefully selected, and the whole force is full of martial spirit. The regiments look upon the neighbouring mountains as their hereditary fighting ground, much in the same way that the border tribes regard the plains as their legitimate field for plunder.

Our most dangerous and important frontier is thus guarded, for many hundred miles, by a force recruited entirely from the martial races on the spot, the authority over them not being in any way vested in the commander-in-chief. There is one exception to this singular arrangement, the apex or key of the whole position being held by a large force of the regular army at Peshawur, in front of the entrance to the celebrated Khyber Pass. This exception, however, merely proves the inconsistency of the scheme. On the one hand, the Punjab Force is divided into two parts, and is not entrusted with the main point of the long line of defence; while, on the other, the general officer at Peshawur finds himself isolated, and with both his flanks guarded by troops over whom he exercises no control, and who may be threatened, or even engaged, almost without his knowledge.

To hold a long and exposed frontier by alien troops raised on the spot, and to the almost total exclusion of English soldiers, is a bold and possibly a dangerous policy; but to increase the risk by a complex division of military authority appears to be a violation of all commonly-received maxims of war. The inconsistency and weakness of the system, however, does not stop here.

In the case of contingents in other parts of India, as they are stationed in provinces within our own dominions, and which are more or less subject to our rule, any irregular action exerted is at all events local; but as the Punjab Force guards an important line of exterior defence, and is under the control of the Lieutenant-Governor of the Province, and as the civil commissioners on the frontier also report direct to him, it follows that, with almost complete military and political power in his hands, a provincial governor is practically entrusted with the conduct of our external relations; and although no active operations can take place without the final sanction of the Supreme Government, it may often happen that to the latter is merely left the barren honour of confirming a course which local action had already rendered inevitable.

There is one other defect to which it is necessary to allude—namely, that as the Punjab Force is thinly scattered along a line extending for several hundred miles, without reserves, it becomes necessary, in the event of war, to concentrate troops at one point, and thus to weaken others at a critical time, because any blow struck by us at one tribe infallibly causes excitement and rouses sympathy all down the border.

From what has been said, it will be apparent that the north-west frontier of India is distinguished by characteristics and features of its own. After a century of progress over apparently interminable plains, until we have marched sixteen hundred miles from Calcutta, we find ourselves holding a few isolated posts at the foot of a rugged precipitous country, inhabited by races of brave men, impregnated with religious antipathies and hereditary habits of plunder. Fond of fighting, for its own sake, and engaged in endless feuds amongst themselves, they are quite ready to forget family quarrels under the superior excitement of a collision with the hated invaders; and, stranger still, they will even for a time put aside religion, race, family feuds and all, and enlist under our flag, knowing that, at all events, the fighting is likely to be serious, and almost certainly will be successful.

Our officers, far removed from the enticements and pleasures

of great cities and of ordinary civilisation, and leading a somewhat sequestered life, find compensation in the varied incidents
and warlike adventures of border service. To live among primi-
tive tribes, who with all their faults and crimes have still manly
virtues, is esteemed preferable to a monotonous career amidst
the enervated and debased races in the lower parts of Bengal.

Chapter 3

The Fanatics of Sitana

With so many elements of disorder already existing on the frontier, it is curious that the campaign on the Mahabun mountain in 1863 should have arisen, in the first instance, from accidental circumstances, with which the tribes of the locality were hardly directly concerned. For many years past a set of violent fanatical outlaws from our own territories, chiefly from the lower provinces of Bengal, many hundred miles distant, had been permitted to reside just over the border, and had settled in a village called 'Sitana,' at the foot of the mountain and on the banks of the Indus—hence their name of Sitana Fanatics. The origin of this colony dates back to the days when Runjeet Sing was ruler of the Punjab, and their history is as follows. Syud Ahmed Shah, the founder, was a native of Bareilly.

At one period of his life he was the companion in arms of the celebrated Ameen Khan Pindaree, who was himself a Pathan, born in the valley of Bonair. Syud Ahmed, having studied Arabic at Delhi, proceeded on a pilgrimage to Mecca by way of Calcutta. It was during this journey that his doctrines obtained the ascendancy over the minds of the Mahomedans of Bengal, which has ever since led them to supply the colony at Sitana with fresh recruits. Although the *Syud* in afterlife attempted to disguise the fact, his doctrines were essentially those of the Wahabee sect, inculcating the original tenets of Islam, and repudiating commentaries on the *Koran*, the adoration of relics, &c.

It was in 1824 that this adventurer arrived amongst the Eusofzye tribes on the Peshawur border, and proclaimed a religious war against the Sikhs. For some years he gained a certain amount of influence among the Pathan races, and in 1829 captured Peshawur; but his exactions became oppressive, many of his followers deserted him, and the remnant were defeated in Hazara in 1830, the *Syud* himself being slain.

Of his disciples who escaped with their lives, a portion found their way to Sitana, where they remained for many years, harboured by the tribes, receiving occasional recruits and money from Lower Bengal, and committing constant depredations in our territories, kidnapping and even murdering peaceable native traders on the highroads. These atrocities reached a climax in 1858, when a small British force, under General Sir Sydney Cotton, was sent against them. The result of this expedition was that the Fanatics were driven off, their several villages destroyed, and engagements were entered into with the neighbouring tribes against their return to Sitana.

Such is a short account of rather a singular colony. As an offspring of religious hate combined with hopes of plunder, it found an appropriate home on the northwest border: but it seems curious that disaffected Mahomedans in our Lower Provinces should imagine that they can shake our power, or accomplish any definite political object, by the feeble device of occasional presents of money and recruits to a nest of outlaws hundreds of miles away, on the confines of Afghanistan; and it is still stranger that those on the spot should, from mere hatred to ourselves, though possibly with a hope of pecuniary advantage, harbour and encourage refugees, whose actions must infallibly sooner or later bring themselves into trouble. The vigorous measures of Sir Sydney Cotton had a powerful but transient effect, and for a time there was peace and quiet on the border; but the Fanatics, who had established themselves in some strength at the village of Mulka, on the north side of the Mahabun mountain, having received money and reinforcements, moved down in 1862, reoccupied Sitana and other neighbouring spots, and recommenced their depredations.

The Mahabun mountain stands on the right bank of the Indus, forty miles above the old fortress of Attock: it is about thirty miles in length from east to west, and as its topmost ridges are little short of 8,000 feet high, it forms an important and striking feature on that part of the frontier. Its sides for the most part are steep, bare, and rugged, the higher summits being fringed with forests of fir, and in the winter capped with snow. There are, however, occasional plateaux of cultivation and numerous small villages belonging to the tribes, and in some parts dense forests run down almost to the plains. The roads are few and bad—in fact, mere mule-tracks between the villages. The mountain on its eastern side is very abrupt, and is divided by the Indus from our province of Hazara; whilst all along, at the foot of its southern slopes, lie the plains of Eusofzye, a portion of the Peshawur district.

Our territories are thus contiguous to it on two faces. A long enclosed valley, called the Chumla, forms its third or north-western front, which is again separated from the large valley of Bonair, still farther north, by an intervening ridge. The only entrance to the Chumla valley is from Eusofzye, by a narrow gorge, a few miles in length, called the Umbeylah Pass; being, in fact, the rocky bed of a little stream, passing round the western side of the Mahabun, and separating the latter from the great Gooroo Mountain. An appreciation of these salient features of the country will render it easy to follow the course of the ensuing military operations.

The scenery from the crest of the Mahabun is very varied, and contains in many respects elements of grandeur. To the south the vast plains of the Punjab stretch away in endless expanse. The Indus, after leaving the foot of the mountain, widens considerably in its southerly course, and at certain seasons attains almost the dimensions of an inland sea. Just before reaching the Kuttuck hills it is joined by the Cabool River, which flows out of the Peshawur valley, and then, passing under the walls of Attock, it rushes through a narrow gorge and is lost to sight. Whilst the chief characteristics of the southern view are those of a vast cultivated plain, watered by large rivers, and dotted here and there with peaceful villages, the aspect to the north is of an entirely different character.

At the very foot of the northern slopes lies the sheltered narrow valley of the Chumla, a rugged spur of the Gooroo rising on its other side, and forming its boundary with Bonair. Beyond this latter valley again, to the north and west, rise still higher peaks and crests on the confines of Swat; and yet again, far away in the distance, great chains of mountains stand up one beyond the other in rugged grandeur, until at length the horizon is closed in by the snowy peaks of the Hindoo Koosh. It is in these distant mountains and in the intervening valleys that the tribes dwell, many of whom, as the rumours of the battles on the Mahabun reached them, at once swarmed down to take part in the attempt to relieve their country of our hated presence.

During the summer of 1863, the blockade of the Mahabun was vigorously carried out by detachments of troops and native levies, at the foot of the mountain on both sides of the Indus. Thus the people of the offending tribes were deprived of access to our markets, and of their ordinary facilities of traffic, a measure often successfully resorted to by us on the frontier, and rendering sometimes further steps of coercion unnecessary. The Fanatics, however, who were actively intriguing with the people in the neighbourhood, not only continued their depredations, but made demonstrations of drilling and parading their men, and fired occasional shots in bravado at our pickets across the river.

CHAPTER 4

The British Government Resolve on a Military Expedition

When the British Government finally decided on measures of military retaliation, the salient position of the Mahabun as regards our own territories, and its comparative isolation from the adjoining ranges, seemed to offer facilities for attacking the fanatics and their abettors without penetrating far over the border, or coming into collision with others. There were, however, difficulties in the case. To march a column up the sides of a steep mountain by dubious paths, when its advent is expected by swarms of resolute mountaineers and fanatics, who have every advantage of ground, and to pass over a crest between seven, and eight thousand feet high, to the attack of a strong village[1] on the northern slope, might no doubt be accomplished; but it is not an easy operation, or one likely to be carried out without considerable loss of life. Besides which, as the retreat of the enemy would still be open to the north, they might fall back as we advanced, and return again as we retired, and thus partially defeat the object of the expedition.

A consideration of the ground, however, seemed to indicate the possibility of an easier and more complete course. The Chumla valley, which, as already explained, lies at the foot of the northern slopes of the Mahabun, communicates with our territory by means of the narrow gorge called the Umbeylah Pass. It

---

1. Mulka.

29

was therefore conceived, that by marching a strong force from Eusofzye rapidly through the pass, and up the valley, it would then occupy an advantageous position, standing between the fanatics and their only line of retreat. The enemy would thus find their position turned instead of being stormed, and our troops could proceed to destroy Mulka, to break up the fanatic force, and to coerce the other tribes. It is true that our own communications might for the moment be endangered, but as it was intended to operate with a column of 5,000 men, the temporary risk would apparently be slight.

Colonel Reynell Taylor, C.B., the Commissioner of the Peshawur district at the time of the expedition, thus speaks of the plan:—

> The prospect held out then by the Chumla route was that, in place of a painful and continued struggle over steep southerly spurs of the Mahabun mountain, the force would be able to take up a position in open ground in rear of the whole tract, which it would fully command, and from whence by rapid excursions it would be able to do all its work, and deal with all its difficulties, returning when convenient to its standing camp in the Chumla plain; while it was obviously and, as experience proved, justly argued, that such a position would render the tribes on the southern slopes well nigh powerless, as their whole position would be stopped, putting them at the mercy of an army which could descend upon their strongholds, and thus carry out its ends with irresistible advantage.

Looking then at the proposal as a purely military movement, and directed solely against an enemy on the Mahabun, it doubtless seemed feasible enough; but as the Chumla valley was only divided by a narrow belt of hills from the country of the Bonairs, it is evident that our force entering by the Umbeylah Pass would arrive at the very threshold of a powerful tribe, whose fighting men numbered, it was supposed, about twelve thousand. The disposition of the Bonairs, therefore, became a serious political consideration, and in reality we knew very little about them.

Mr. Temple, in his report already noticed, speaks of them as follows:—

> Beyond the Judoon country, on the north-west, is Boonere, or Bunoor. It is a rugged country, extending from the lower range of the Hindoo Koosh downwards, to hills which command the Chumla valley and the central plain of Eusofzye. On its western frontier, again, lies the Swat territory. The Boonere people are strong; they could muster a force of some thousands: they appear to be on good terms with the Swatees. In 1849 they aided some British subjects at Loondkhoor in Eusofzye, who refused to pay revenue; but they have generally abstained from molesting our subjects, and we have had no concern with them.

Colonel Taylor wrote:—

> The Bonair people had no sympathy as a body with the Fanatics, being of different tenets, and forming part of the religious constituency of the *Akhoond* of Swat, who was known to be bitterly opposed at that time to the Fanatic body, the members of which he denounced as Wahabees, coupling them with his especial rival the Kotah Moollah, whom with his disciples he had not scrupled to stigmatise as Kaffirs, *i. e. infidels*, for certain heterodox theories opposed to his (the *Akhoond's*) rulings in matters affecting the Mahomedan faith.
>
> It was, indeed, known that the Sitana Fanatics had on several occasions paraded detachments of men with standards, &c., from Bonair; but small importance was attached to the fact, as it was known to be their custom to purchase the services of idle tribesmen, to parade them for their own purposes; and had it been supposed that men had really been sent as auxiliaries by a portion of the tribe, it would have been considered that they must belong to the Kotah Moollah's faction, and therefore be acting contrary to the general sense and politics of the tribes. . . . I think

I am justified in saying, that although there had been rumours of overtures attempted on one side, nothing at that
time was, to all appearance, so little probable as a coalition
between the *Akhoond* of Swat and his adherents and the
Hindostanees. . . .

When, therefore, it became apparent that the route proposed for the force would take it only through a valley
adjoining Bonair, but divided from it by a range of mountains, our professed and known object being to punish a
body of men whom the *Akhoond*, the religious leader of
the Bonair people, had denounced, and expressly declared
that he would not aid or support, the contingency of the
Bonair tribe taking up the cause seemed scarcely, as the
expression is, "on the cards;" and though occasionally dis-
cussed, it was dismissed as highly improbable.

It was, under the circumstances, impossible to examine
the proposed route by questioning those of our own territories best acquainted with it, without raising suspicions
as to the line we proposed to take in entering the hills;
and, for the same reason, it was not advisable to consult
the Bonair *jirgah* or tribe-council. Had we questioned our
own Suddhoom chiefs, the men who knew most about
the clan and the Chumla valley, it is little to be doubted
that an inkling obtained by them of our intentions would
assuredly have been communicated to Bonair and Chumla; and the result we knew would have been a serious opposition to our first day's march, which we believed would
not have been raised, or, if suggested, would be abandoned
as useless, when we had cracked the nut, by passing the
defile, and placed ourselves in the Chumla plain.

The general conclusion, apparently, arrived at by the Lahore
Government was that, although little was known of the Bonairs,
their general disposition to us was rather friendly than other-
wise, and the proposed movement through the Umbeylah Pass
was therefore decided on. But there is another feature in the case
which must be noticed, that, however ready we were to rely on

the apathy of the Bonairs, we carefully concealed from them our plan of operations. This may have been judicious, but was hardly a friendly act on our part. We were about to march by a circuitous route to accomplish our object on the Mahabun, and yet we purposely omitted to inform a powerful tribe whose valley lay in the immediate vicinity of our line of march.

General Chamberlain's first despatch, after entering the Umbeylah Pass, says:—

I should here mention that on the afternoon of the 19th,[1] when it would be too late for the Chumla or other tribes to make any preparations on a large scale for impeding the march of the troops through the Umbeylah Pass, a proclamation was forwarded by the Commissioner to the Chumla and Bonair tribes, stating the object with which the force was about to enter the Chumla valley, and assuring them that it was with no intention of injuring them, or of interfering with their independence, but solely because it was the most convenient route by which to reach the Hindostanee fanatics, and to effect their expulsion from the Mahabun.

But the question was, in what light were the Bonairs likely to regard our sudden and unexpected arrival at the door of their house, our purpose having been carefully hid until the time for their objecting or defending themselves had passed away?

The late Major James, who was the commissioner when peace was made, alluding to these circumstances writes:

Even supposing, therefore, that the proclamations actually reached their destination, was it likely that a brave race of ignorant men would pause to consider the purport of a paper they could not read, when the arms of a supposed invader were glistening at their doors?

Knowing the jealous dislike which all the mountain tribes have to our entering their territory at any time, we could hard-

---

1. October 19, 1863.

ly expect they should view our proceedings with indifference; and it so happens that in this instance (as was afterwards discovered), their suspicions of our good faith had already been excited. When the Fanatics first heard of the assembly of our troops in Eusofzye, and thus became aware that we were about to call them to account, although they did not divine our actual plan, they nevertheless wrote a very crafty letter to the Bonairs, endeavouring to enlist their support. This letter subsequently fell into our hands, and the chief parts of it are as follows:—

> The evil-doing *infidels* will plunder and devastate the whole of the hilly tract— especially the provinces of Chumla, Bonair, Swat, &c.—and annex these countries to their dominions, and then our religion and worldly possessions would entirely be subverted. Consequently, keeping in consideration a regard for Islam, the dictates of faith and worldly affairs, you ought by no means to neglect the opportunity. The *infidels* are extremely deceitful and treacherous, and will, by whatever means they can, come into these hills, and declare to the people of the country that they have no concerns with them, that their quarrel is with the Hindostanees, that they will not molest the people, even as much as touch a hair of their heads, but will return immediately after having extirpated the Hindostanees, and that they will not interfere with their country. They will also tempt the people with wealth. It is therefore proper for you not to give in to their deceit, or else, when they should get an opportunity, they will entirely ruin, torment, and put you to many indignities, appropriate to themselves your entire wealth and possessions, and injure your faith. You will then obtain nothing but regret. We impress this matter on your attention.

Our stealthy march and unexpected arrival at the head of the Umbeylah Pass, therefore, tended to confirm all that the Fanatics had predicted; the worst suspicions of the Bonairs were aroused, and our forced delay in the gorge, which will be related hereafter, determined them to oppose us with all their might, and to call upon the whole of the frontier tribes to support them. It is important that the facts relating to this part of the subject should be clearly understood, because the result of the Bonair opposition was to convert a small expedition into a frontier war, which required time, money, and hard fighting to bring to a successful issue.

Chapter 5

Views of Lord Elgin on the War

On the 15th of September, the Lieutenant-Governor of the Punjab addressed the Viceroy at Simla, recapitulating the history of the Sitana Fanatics, and requesting authority for a force of 5,000 men to march into the mountains. It was supposed that the expedition would last about three weeks, and it was advisable that it should start early in October, as the intense cold of the early winter in the mountains, and the possible fall of snow at the latter part of November, might be injurious to the troops. As some of the regiments would have to be summoned from distant points on the frontier, the Lieutenant-Governor requested and obtained sanction for the expedition, in the first instance, by telegraph.

The general views of Lord Elgin, the Viceroy, are stated as follows:—

It was the anxious desire of the Governor-General that peace should, if possible, be maintained on the Hazara frontier; but the overt acts of hostility which have taken place since the Fanatics, contrary to the engagements entered into by the Judoon and Otmanzai tribes, have been suffered to reoccupy Sitana and other parts on the right bank of the Indus, impose the necessity of repressing and punishing such wanton aggressions. The Lieutenant-Governor has called the attention of His Excellency to the fact, that whereas, hitherto, the hostilities or provocation had been offered by detached tribes, it was now for the

first time that the majority, if not the whole, of the Hazara border-tribes were arrayed against the British Government, and that it was reported that overtures had been
made to the *Akhoond* of Swat.

After the hostile acts already perpetrated, it is to be expected that the Hindostanee Fanatics and their allies
should seek to extend the coalition to tribes of greater
strength than those as yet more or less committed: His Excellency feels compelled, therefore, whilst the circle of the
leagued tribes is still of contracted area and of manage-
able dimensions, to have recourse to military operations,
with a view to the expulsion of the Hindostanee Fanatics,
the punishment of the committed tribes, the exaction of
sufficient guarantees for the future maintenance of peace
and good order on our frontiers, and a timely prevention
of the spread of disturbance over a larger area, by the de-
terring effect which active and adequate operations may
produce at the present juncture.

To fulfil these objects, the Governor-General consid-
ers that the force to be employed should not be less in
strength than that asked for by the Lieutenant-Governor—*viz.* 5,000 infantry, with a proportionate and suitable
equipment of artillery, and some cavalry. A force of the
proposed strength should be able to carry out the objects
of the expedition.

The decision of Government to undertake a war beyond the
frontier was at the same time communicated to the commander-
in-chief in India. It is necessary, however, to observe that the important flank movement towards Bonair was not decided on by
the Lieutenant-Governor of the Punjab until a later period, just
previous to the march of the column. On the general question
of a war beyond the border, Sir Hugh Rose, the commander-
in-chief, lost no time in advising the Government. He pointed
out the danger of denuding Peshawur and other stations on the
frontier of troops and of means of transport, at the very moment
when, by entering the mountains at one point, we should create

excitement along the whole line.

He further brought to notice, that considerable preparations were necessary for the due equipment of a force of 5,000 men, intended to enter a hostile, difficult, and unknown country, as regards supplies, transport, ammunition, &c.; that the time allowed was insufficient, and also that the period available for active operations was very short. Sir Hugh Rose deprecated more hasty flying-marches through the mountains, arguing that the results of former expeditions had been unsatisfactory, and had not produced the intended effect of awing the tribes. He therefore proposed that the disturbed frontier should be vigorously blockaded till the spring, when a well-arranged expedition could be formed to carry out the views of Government.

Sir Hugh Rose's advice was disregarded, and the force was ordered to proceed; but it is remarkable, that no sooner had our troops entered the mountains, than each one of his representations was successively vindicated and confirmed, day after day, by the telegrams and letters received from the General Officer in command. Additional regiments were required at once, but could only be sent in the first instance from Peshawur, which had already been drawn upon, and which itself was threatened soon afterwards. More English officers and medical men were asked for, as well as supplies, ammunition, medical stores, and boots, &c. The transport arrangements were reported as defective; consequently, the road in the pass became blocked up with animals and baggage; and thus the force was compelled to halt at the end of the first day's march, which confirmed the Bonairs in their hostility. A general combination of the tribes ensued, and the excitement spread all down the frontier.

Considering the hasty manner in which the expedition was organised, the very difficult country to be operated in, and the powerful combination which the force had to fight against, the Government were most fortunate in their selection of the officer appointed to the command. Sir Neville Chamberlain's great name, his long experience, and his well-known brave and chivalrous character, were indeed sufficient guarantees of the ultimate success of our arms; and it is a happy circumstance that in the serious complications and hard battles which ensued, a man of such rare energy and never-failing courage should have been at the head of affairs; and although he was struck down by a severe wound before the operations were quite at an end, it may be admitted, without disparagement to his successor, that the neck of the confederacy had already in great measure been broken by the vigorous blows struck by General Chamberlain, and that the tribes were sick at heart and almost weary of the contest.

It is not possible, in this account, to give even an outline of the interesting and remarkable services of General Chamberlain in India during the last quarter of a century. Suffice it to say that he has taken a distinguished part in almost every campaign, that he has been repeatedly wounded, and that his name is a terror to the enemies of England throughout the border. His whole career, indeed, affords a bright example of true devotion and of modest courage.

CHAPTER 6

Difficulties of Mountain Warfare

Offensive mountain warfare, in a hostile unknown region, is the prosecution of a difficult art under most trying circumstances. All the ordinary obstructions to successful campaigning then present themselves in an aggravated form. Whether in climbing steep ridges, or in forcing rocky defiles, the advantages of ground and the knowledge of locality are entirely in favour of the enemy. They not only hold all the commanding points, but the very habits of their daily life render them peculiarly adapted for irregular fighting. Simple and abstemious in their living, the air and exercise on the mountain-side inure them to hardships, and render them capable of great physical exertion. The well-fed soldiers of the plains, on the other hand, toiling wearily over, the unwonted difficulties of the ground, find that the advantages of their regular formations and severe drill are of little avail under conditions so antagonistic to ordinary routine.

But the difficulties of moving large and regularly-organised bodies of men, over a steep and almost pathless country do not end here. The transport required for the carriage of food, ammunition, clothing, medical stores, and the hundred details which go to meet the almost artificial wants of modern armies, render rapid locomotion nearly impossible, and our Indian experience has hitherto been very adverse to lightness of equipment.

For a century past, indeed, our troops have wandered slowly and wearily over the interminable plains, followed by long lines of elephants, camels, bullocks, and carts, transporting huge tents, together with tables, chairs, bedsteads, carpets, crockery, and many other unwieldy and unnecessary items of officers' and soldiers' equipment; and to these *impedimenta* must be added the hordes of native followers, who, far outnumbering the fighting men, have been and still are the invariable appendage of an Indian army. So that now when we have arrived at the foot of a mountainous tract, where every additional pound of weight is an obstruction, and every extra mouth to feed a difficulty, our traditional habits, bad enough before, render us peculiarly unfitted to encounter the novel circumstances of the case.

An experience of twenty years on the frontier has so far been beneficial, that the Punjab local regiments are provided with mule-transport, and are fairly adapted for quick movement, though even with them baggage is by no means reduced to a minimum; but as the majority of General Chamberlain's column was composed of the regular troops, who are not so equipped, rapid marching was unlikely to be realised.

The Lahore Government, indeed, authorised the hire of camels and pack-mules in considerable numbers, as best adapted for the contingency; but the mere hasty collection of animals never can constitute an effective transport corps, nor are the rigid necessities of mountain warfare likely to be thoroughly appreciated in a moment, by officers accustomed to the cumbrous proportions of Oriental *impedimenta*. So that although General Chamberlain, from long experience, was fully alive to the inconvenience, and although rapidity of execution was almost a necessity to the success of the projected campaign, the animals that followed in his line of march were numbered by thousands, and the narrow gorge of the Umbeylah Pass became blocked up, thus rendering advance for the time impossible; and there are many officers who believe that this enforced inaction of several days at the outset was the final cause which determined the Bonair hostility, and the consequent combination of the tribes against us.

During the early part of October, the troops intended for the operations were assembled in Eusofzye, some coming from

Peshawur, and others from distant frontier stations. The force consisted, in round numbers, of about 5,000 men (of whom one-fourth were English soldiers) and eleven guns.

The details are as follows:—

TROOPS OF THE REGULAR ARMY.

½ Battery Royal Artillery. 3 Guns on elephants.
71st Highland Light Infantry.
101st Royal Bengal Fusiliers.
2 Companies of Native Sappers.
20th Regiment of Native Infantry.
32nd Regiment of Native Infantry.
11th Bengal Native Cavalry.

PUNJAB IRREGULAR FORCE

2 Native Mountain Batteries. 8 small Guns on muleback.
Regiment of Guides, Native Infantry.
1st, 3rd, 5th, and 6th Regiments of Native Infantry.
5th Goorkhas.
Guide Cavalry.

On October 18th the column advanced across Eusofzye towards the foot of the Mahabun; and in order to deceive the enemy, a feint was made in the direction of the road by which Sir Sydney Cotton had ascended the mountain in 1858, so as to convey the impression that the same course would be followed again.

On the 19th a proclamation was issued to the Bonairs and other tribes, informing them that the British force was about to enter the Mahabun tract to punish the Fanatics and their abettors; and that the intentions of Government were thus made known, so that the friendly tribes might be under no anxiety as to their own possessions.

On the morning of the 20th, the advance-guard entered the Umbeylah Pass, and, meeting with trivial opposition, arrived the same afternoon near its other extremity, just where it begins to open the Chumla valley, the entrance to which latter was thus secured, and the main body followed in the course of the day.

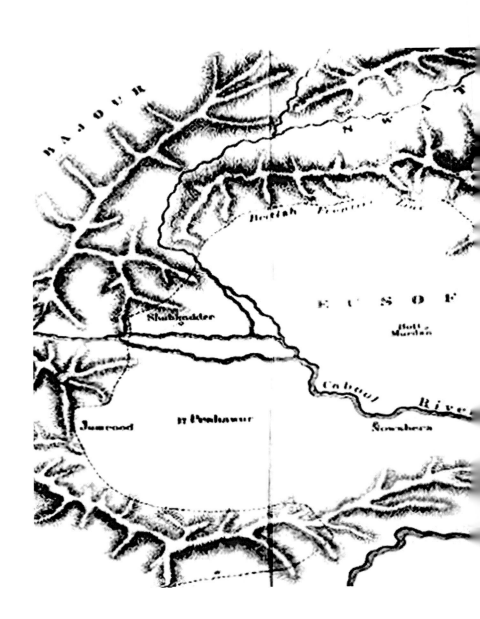

Sketch Map of the Mountains round
THE PESHAWUR VALLEY.

━━ Position of the British force in
     the Umbeylah Pass.

Scale of Miles.

The length of the actual pass is about nine miles.
General Chamberlain says:

As a road for troops it certainly presents great difficulties.
The track lies up the bed of a stream encumbered with
boulders and large masses of rock, and is overgrown with
low trees and jungle. The hills on either side rise to some
height but for the most part with a gradual slope, so that
infantry can ascend them without difficulty, except for the
obstacle presented by thick thorny jungle. The guns were
drawn by horses as far as possible, and then transferred to
elephants. The progress of the force was of course extremely slow, as in most parts it was only practicable to move in
single file, and the British troops were much fatigued; but
the plentiful stream of water which flows through the pass
prevented their suffering from thirst.

CHAPTER 7

Attack of the Bonairs

The position taken up by the force, at the end of their first day's march, was in the bed of a rocky stream; the Gooroo, a lofty mountain 6,000 feet high, rising up on the left, whilst the steep slopes of the Mahabun formed a similar barrier on the other side. Both mountains were clothed with forests of fir of large growth, whilst here and there open spaces and rocky knolls formed convenient spots for our pickets.[1] To the front of the camp the pass gradually widened, and merged into the Chumla valley, which was apparently well cultivated, and with a small stream flowing through it. Near its entrance stood the large village of Umbeylah, about three miles distant, with the hills of Bonair above and to its left. In the far distance to the rear, looking down the gorge, were the plains of Eusofzye.

This position was certainly not a desirable one to hold for any length of time, either in a military or political sense, and the intention had been to push on without delay. But, as General Chamberlain writes,

> When I found what difficulties the pass presented even to the march of troops, and how long it would necessarily be before the whole of the baggage could come up, I thought it prudent to make no farther movement in advance. The ammunition mules of the infantry had been able with difficulty to keep up with the rear of their respective regi-

---

1. *Vide* Frontispiece.

ments, but, with this exception, not a single baggage animal reached the camp during the night of the 20th.

For the same reason, the whole of the next day was passed in inaction. The obstructions in the road, the great amount and inferior nature of the transport, and the incompetence of the drivers, caused dangerous delay; so that it was not until the afternoon of the 22nd that a reconnoitring party, escorted by a small body of light cavalry, was pushed on into the Chumla valley. The first village approached was that of Umbeylah, which, although not in their immediate territory, belongs to the Bonairs; and the party, with a view to avoid giving offence, did not enter it, but passed up, meeting no opposition, to the village of Kooria, at the other extremity of the valley, about seven or eight miles farther on.

It had been observed, however, that the hills to the left and immediately above Umbeylah were held in force by the Bonairs; and on the return of the reconnoitring party a large body of men moved down to cut off their retreat, and opened fire. In self-defence the cavalry then charged, killing a few of the enemy. The Bonairs followed them with great determination, and endeavoured to close sword in hand with a party of infantry who covered the return to our position in the pass: The night closed in; but the Bonairs, apparently exasperated and determined to fight, continued a general desultory attack on all parts of our camp until midnight, killing Lieutenant Gillies, of the Royal Artillery, and causing a few other casualties.

These events of October 22nd were in every way serious. General Chamberlain was standing in a deep gorge, with huge mountains on either side, and with a narrow defile, nine miles long, blocked up with baggage animals, between him and the plains of Eusofzye; whilst on his left front a powerful tribe, with whom we had no cause of quarrel whatever, had suddenly broken out into war. The intended advance on Mulka was not only delayed, but became of secondary importance in the face of the altered position of affairs; a considerable complication as the result of one day's march into the mountains.

The general's despatch of the 23rd clearly explains the whole matter, and shows that he fully appreciated the serious nature of the case:—

The Bonair people (he says) having thus taken a decidedly hostile part against us, is extremely serious, and has altered our whole position, and probably our plan of operations. That their conduct has been prompted by the Hindostanee fanatics at Sitana there can be no doubt. Some papers have been intercepted, which show that ever since it became known that the present expedition was being organised against them, the Hindostanees have been endeavouring to obtain the assistance of the people of Bonair, by alarming them as to our intentions of annexing their country. The hostility of Bonair must now be considered as a fact, and our course of action guided accordingly. Its probable effect upon the security of our communications has first to be considered and guarded against.

In this view I have ordered up the wing of the 14th Native Infantry from Nowakilla to Roostum, and applied for another native infantry regiment to be sent from Peshawur. I have requested the Commissioner to arrange for the occupation of the lower portion of the pass with his foot levies, and it is probable that I shall have to ask for more native infantry, before the communication with the rear can be considered secure, even so long as the force occupies its present position on the crest of the Umbeylah Pass.

His Excellency is in possession of my original plan of operations, namely, to use the Chumla valley as a route for reaching the Hindostanee settlements on the Mahabun. But with a powerful and warlike tribe, like the people of Bonair, in declared hostility on the left flank of our proposed line of march, and in a position to which they can always return, even though once dislodged and beaten, it may now be impossible to persevere in this plan of operations. Besides, our latest information is to the effect, that the Bonair people have summoned the Hindostanees to their aid, and that a portion of them at least have obeyed the summons.

It is doubtful, therefore, whether the original object in view can now be obtained by the force penetrating to the Mahabun, and whether the Hindostanee Fanatics will not be either encountered in our present position fighting with the people of Bonair, or have to be sought elsewhere than on the spurs of the Mahabun.

Again, writing on October 25th, he says:—

There appears to be reason to believe that the Bonair people have applied to the *Akhoond* of Swat for aid; and should they succeed in enlisting him in their cause, which is not improbable, as they are his spiritual followers, the object with which this force took the road of the Chumla valley would be still more difficult of attainment. The influence of the *Akhoond* of Swat over all the hill and plain tribes on the Peshawur frontier is very great, and towards them he fills a position which I can best illustrate by comparing it with that of the Pope of Rome. If he declare against us, he will no doubt bring an immense accession of material as well as moral strength to the people of Bonair and the other tribes already in arms against us.

It will be found that, in a few days, these anticipations as regards the *Akhoond* were fully verified, and that he arrived in person with several thousand followers, took up his position on the crest of the Bonair hills, overlooking Umbeylah, and also summoned the men of other distant tribes to join the cause.

CHAPTER 8

Gallantry of Our Native Troops

General Chamberlain now took measures to clear himself of encumbrances, and to prepare for hard fighting. The sick, the baggage, and the spare transport animals were sent back to the plains, and the road was improved. A breastwork was thrown across the front of the camp, and flanked with guns; the steep slopes on either side were occupied by strong pickets, stockaded, and entrenched. Still the position was weak; the flanks were necessarily extended far up the mountain-sides, and therefore reinforcements could only reach them slowly, and after a fatiguing ascent.[1] The extreme left picket on the Gooroo Mountain, named the 'Eagle's Nest,' stood on a rocky projecting knoll far above the camp.

That on the right, called the 'Crag Picket,' was equally commanding, and towered up into the sky, a pinnacle of huge rocks scantily clothed with pines. Both were vital points to hold, for they entirely overlooked the lower defences. But, high as they both were, there were other ridges and dominant points still far above them; and our troops were thus exposed to sudden and overwhelming attacks from enemies who could assemble unseen and at their leisure on the mountain crests, and choose their time for a crushing assault. Fortunately, there were many officers with the force as undaunted in spirit as the general himself, and who with unflinching tenacity held on to the rocky knolls which were given them to defend.

---

1. *Vide* Frontispiece.

The men of the tribes were brave and worthy foes. These bold mountaineers, ignorant of discipline or of any regular art of war, armed only with rude matchlocks and short swords, nevertheless, by a kind of natural instinct, discovered at once our weak points; and by feints at the centre, combined with furious assaults on the isolated flanks, not only inflicted heavy loss upon us, but succeeded occasionally in endangering the whole position. The Crag Picket alone fell three times into their hands, by direct assault, at different periods of the campaign.

In describing the various actions, which for the next month followed each other in rapid succession, several extracts are quoted from the despatches of those engaged, because, though hastily written on the spot, their freshness gives a vivid reality to the scenes depicted.

On October 24th, large bodies of men, with numerous standards, appeared in the Chumla valley, and were ascertained to be arrivals from some of the minor hill tribes, and a portion of the Fanatics under Mobarik Shah. At daylight the next morning, these reinforcements appeared above our right defences on the Mahabun, but were driven off by Major Keyes,[2] who chased them vigorously along the ridges, and forced them back precipitately into the valley.

The events of the following day (October 26) were serious. General Chamberlain, having some reason to apprehend an attack on the Eagle's Nest, reinforced the troops on the Gooroo Mountain, sending up 200 men of the 71st Highlanders, the 5th and 6th Punjab Regiments, and a mountain battery. The Eagle's Nest itself and the adjacent rocks were held by 230 men, chiefly marksmen of various corps, under Major Brownlow.[3]

The enemy, who had established a breastwork of their own on the heights above, and were in great strength, no sooner observed our preparations for battle than they joyfully accepted the challenge. The scene is well described by Colonel Vaughan, who was in command:—

2. Later Lieutenant-Colonel Keyes, C B., commanding the 1st Punjab Infantry.
3. Later Lieutenant-Colonel Brownlow, C.B., commanding the 20th Native Infantry.

The troops were hardly in position when a very large body of the enemy rushed down the steep slopes of the mountain above, and with loud cries attacked at once the picket and the troops. The mountain-train guns fired upon the enemy with shrapnel, common shell, and round-shot; and this fire checked those who were advancing against the troops in position, but not those advancing against the picket. The latter was attacked with the greatest determination, and two of the enemy's standards were planted close under the parapet which crowns the steep sides of the picket hill.

All the efforts of the picket failed to dislodge the enemy from the position for some time, notwithstanding that the direct fire from the picket was aided by a flanking fire from the mountain-train guns and from the Enfield rifles of the 71st. But as the attack upon the picket will form the subject of a separate report from Major Brownlow, I shall only remark here, that so desperately was it attacked, and so hardly was it pressed, that it became necessary for me to reinforce it in the course of the action with the company of the 71st Highland Light Infantry, and a company of the 5th Punjab Infantry. When the enemy had been checked by the guns, they were charged by the 6th Punjab Infantry, but the regiment was unfortunately carried too far in the ardour of pursuit, and lost heavily before it could regain the position.

Whilst this fierce struggle was taking place on the steep mountain-side, and whilst the echoes were ringing with the shouts of the combatants and the unwonted discharge of artillery, Major Brownlow was standing at bay behind a small breastwork in the Eagle's Nest; and he gives a simple and vivid account of the attack upon him:—

About 12 o'clock (noon), the Bonairwals, who had hitherto fired only an occasional shot, commenced to move down from their position, matchlock-men posting themselves most advantageously in the wood, and opening a very galling fire upon us; while their swordsmen and others advanced boldly to the attack, charging across the plateau in our front in the most determined manner, and planting their standard behind a rock within a few feet of our wall. The steady fire, however, with which they were received, rendered their very gallant efforts to enter our defences unavailing, and they were driven back and up the hill, leaving the ground covered with their dead; their matchlock-men only maintaining the fight, and continuing to harass us much.

Our losses in this first great attack of the Bonairs were severe. Two brave young officers—Lieutenants Richmond, of the 20th Regiment, and Clifford, of the 3rd Punjab Infantry—fell whilst encouraging their men; and an old native officer, Subadar-Major Meer Ally Shah, died like a gallant soldier at his commanding-officer's side, recommending his son to Major Brown- low's protection. Two English and no less than nine native officers were wounded, and the list of casualties, altogether, amounted to 130.

The great losses incurred by the native corps in this, as in every action during the campaign, are a proof of the loyalty of the men to our cause; and the records of those who subsequently received the 'Order of Merit' from Government, afford bright instances of personal devotion. In this attack, for instance, one native officer is rewarded for having led his company under a heavy fire, and when his commanding-officer was struck down, having remained to defend him, and saved his life. The conspicuous gallantry of another soldier is mentioned, as rushing ahead of his corps, cutting down a standard-bearer, and capturing the standard. Many other cases might be quoted.

It ought to be observed, that the great majority of the native soldiers employed in this war were either Sikhs or men of the northern Pathan tribes; men who in character, courage, and manly bearing, present a marked contrast to the enervated races of the lower parts of Bengal. Indeed, it is a remarkable fact that, as we ascend to the North-west, the inhabitants seem gradually but very perceptibly to improve, so that in the higher parts of India we have a never-failing source of supply of good soldiers, although, from their strong religious and national feelings, there may be a danger in employing them too exclusively in their own part of the country. General Chamberlain, in his despatches, bears warm testimony to their devotion during the war; and points out that, although there were men in the native regiments of almost every tribe on the frontier, including those which were fighting against us, still there were no desertions, nor was there any instance of backwardness in engaging the enemy.

CHAPTER 9

Alarming Development of the War

On the day following the great fight at the 'Eagle's Nest,' the Bonairs, who had lost many men, obtained permission to carry off their dead. They were courteous and unreserved in their demeanour on that occasion, but did not appear in the least humbled by their defeat. For a few days subsequently there was a lull in the attacks of the enemy; but the storm soon gathered again, and important events followed each other in rapid succession.

General Chamberlain's despatch of October 31st gives an able historical summary of the alarming development of the war, which deserves careful consideration; and he also explains why, in the face of a powerful combination of the tribes against us, he was unable to advance and carry out the designs of Government.

In my letter of the 25th instant (he says), I mentioned that the people of Bonair had applied to the *Akhoond* of Swat, to aid them in resisting the advance of the force, and stated my opinion that, in the event of his doing so, the object with which the force had adopted the route of the Chumla valley would, of course, be rendered very difficult of attainment. I have now to report that the *Akhoond* has actually joined the Bonairs, and that he has brought with him upwards of 100 standards from Swat, each standard representing, probably, from twenty to thirty footmen; and, it is said, 120 horsemen.

Besides the tribe with which he is more immediately connected, *viz.* the Swatees, he has summoned the people of the remote country of the Bajour, on the border of the Cabool territory, the Mullazyes of Dher, under their chief Ghuzzan Khan, and other distant tribes, whose names even are hardly known, except to the officers who have served long on the frontiers. There is, in fact, a general combination of almost all the tribes, from the Indus to the boundary of Cabool, against us.

Old animosities are, for the time, in abeyance; and under the influence of fanaticism, tribes usually hostile to each other are hastening to join the *Akhoond's* standard, and to fight for the sake of their common faith. The *Akhoond* has hitherto been opposed to the Sitana Moolvie, who represents an exceptional sect of Mahomedans; but at present the two are understood to be on friendly terms, and it is certain that the whole of the Hindostanee colony are either at, or on their way to, Umbeylah.

It is necessary that I should place the state of affairs thus distinctly before His Excellency, in order that he may understand how entirely the situation has altered since the force entered the Umbeylah Pass; and that, instead of having to deal with the Mahabun tribes, with a view to the expulsion of the Hindostanees from that mountain, we are engaged in a contest in which not only are the Hindostanees and the Mahabun tribes, but also the Swatees, the Bajourees, and the Indus tribes north of the Burrendo, with a large sprinkling of the discontented and restless spirits from within our own border.

I feel certain that His Excellency will approve of my not making an advance into the Chumla valley, with my present force, in the face of the above coalition. I could only do so by giving up the Umbeylah Pass. If the force moved into the valley with a view to continue its advance towards the Mahabun, and to carry out the original views of the Government, it would be exposed to the enemy's incessant attacks, both by night and day, in flank and rear;

and it would be impossible, in the face of such numbers, to protect adequately a long line of laden animals, to which would be added daily an ever-increasing number of sick and wounded.

On the other hand, if the force merely moved into the valley with a view to take up a position in the open ground, it would still lose its communication with the rear; and whenever it required fresh supplies of provisions or ammunition, or to clear the camp by sending sick and wounded to the rear, it would have to retake the pass, and to reoccupy, at great sacrifice of life, the very ground from which it had advanced.

Further, I have felt it right not to forget, that if this force should be seriously compromised by a hazardous movement in advance, there are not, within a very great distance, the troops necessary to meet any difficulty, which would be certain, under such an eventuality, immediately to arise either within or beyond the border. In fact, my judgment tells me that, with our present numbers, the only way to uphold the honour of our arms and the interests of the Government is to act on the defensive, in the position the force now holds, and trust to the effect of time, and of the discouragement which repeated unsuccessful attacks are likely to produce upon the enemy, to weaken their numbers and to break up their combination.

The first result of the combination between the *Akhoond* and the *Moolvie* was an attack upon the right pickets of the camp, early yesterday morning, by the Hindostanees, and an almost simultaneous attack upon the front of the camp by the Swatees. The front attack was repulsed, under my personal superintendence, without difficulty, by the good practice of the artillery under Captain Tulloh, and the fire of Her Majesty's 71st Highland Light Infantry, and the 101st Royal Bengal Fusiliers, which lined the breast-works, under Colonel Hope, C.B., and Lieutenant-Colonel Salusbury, respectively. Some of the enemy behaved with considerable boldness, and afforded an opportunity for the 5th Goorkha Regiment to make a spirited charge. They left forty dead bodies on the field, which have been recognised as men from Swat and Raneezye; and must have lost heavily in addition, though, according to custom, they carried off as many of their dead as they could.

The attack by the Hindostanees on the right was directed against the extreme right picket, known as the Crag. A little before daylight the picket was attacked in force by the enemy, and its garrison driven in. It was, however, brilliantly retaken by Major C. P. Keyes, commanding the 1st Punjab Infantry, as soon as the day broke, at a loss to the enemy of nearly sixty killed.

The rapid development of the war, the great accessions of strength which the enemy were receiving, and the constant attacks upon our position in the pass, rendered it necessary to reinforce General Chamberlain without loss of time. The 14th Ferozepore Native Infantry, the 4th Goorkhas from Peshawur, and two field-guns of a native Punjab battery, joined him towards the end of October, and additional supplies of ammunition and medical stores, &c, were sent from Peshawur, but it was evident that these measures were insufficient.

On October 27th Chamberlain had telegraphed as follows:

All goes well, and I entertain no fear as to final result, if supported by more infantry, and kept in supplies and ammunition. Tribes losing men, and will tire first. The *Akhoond* of Swat having joined coalition is serious, because his influence extends as far as Kohat, and other tribes may take up the fanatical cry. I recommend your sending Trans-Indus as many troops as can be spared from below. Any backwardness now might cause great inconvenience, whereas, if the tribes hear of the arrival of troops, those tribes not committed are likely to keep quiet.

This was a serious state of affairs, and the Government of the Punjab, now fully alive to the fact that what they had originally looked upon as a mere mountain excursion, had assumed the alarming proportions of a frontier war, were anxious that a reserve brigade should be formed to support General Chamberlain. This, however, was a matter of time and of difficulty, as all the northern military stations had been already weakened in forming the expedition, and even at Lahore, the capital of the province, there were few available troops. At the same time the General Officer at Peshawur reported that part of the frontier was in a very uneasy state, and asked for reinforcements; and he also found it necessary to organise a moveable column of horse artillery and cavalry, so as to be ready to check casual incursions into the district.

The Government, indeed, were becoming seriously concerned at the unexpected turn of events. There was political and military danger in standing still in the Umbeylah Pass, whilst, at the same time, any advance into Bonair might lead to still farther complications, and to a war of long duration. The question was undoubtedly a difficult one to solve, and for some time the Government, apparently unwilling to realise the facts, clung to their original decision of going to Mulka. They desired, in short, to strike a blow, if possible, and to come out of the mountains. In the abstract this was natural enough, but General Chamberlain, with a powerful combination on his left flank, reasonably enough deprecated advancing on Mulka, and leaving his communications at the mercy of his enemies. The only resource therefore was to remain on the defensive, and wait for reinforcements.

CHAPTER 10

The Enemy Renew Their Attacks

From the description already given of the position of our force in the gorge, it will be evident that, with an enemy in partial possession of the mountains on both sides, our communications with Eusofyze were somewhat precarious, and liable at any time to interruption. With a view, therefore, to render us independent of the Umbeylah Pass, and to make the route to the plains more secure, a road was commenced from our right defences to the rear, over the slopes of the Mahabun; and in the same way, in order to facilitate an advance when it should become advisable, a second rough path was commenced to the front, down one of the rocky spurs of the same mountain running into the Chumla valley.

The tribes, as usual, watched these proceedings with great jealousy, and the ground in front enabled them to harass our people; and on November 6 they succeeded in partially cutting off a party, which had been sent out to cover the workmen. In order to understand how this occurred, it must be explained that the Mahabun runs down to the Chumla valley in a series of steep, almost parallel, rough spurs, which are partly covered with firs, and encumbered with enormous rocks; and the intervening ravines are so deep and precipitous, that to protect the workmen on one ridge it was necessary to detach armed parties to those beyond. The result of this was that the covering parties, although their actual distance from camp was not great, were very isolated; as, owing to the ravines, it was almost impossible to communicate with or reinforce them, except by first ascending the mountain, and then passing down the particular ridge on which they were posted.

On the day in question, Major G. Harding, of the Bombay Staff Corps, was in command of these outlying pickets; and the enemy, by creeping up under cover of the ground, which in every way facilitated their movements, succeeded in partially surrounding him. An order had been sent early in the afternoon for the withdrawal of the party, and later, when it became evident that he was seriously attacked, supports were sent to meet him at the crest of the mountain, and a regiment of Goorkhas also attempted to reach him across the ridges. The greater part of Major Harding's men eventually reached camp, under cover of the night, but that gallant officer—who, it is supposed, had delayed his return from a chivalrous desire to bring home his wounded—was killed. Ensign Murray, of the 71st, and Lieutenant Dougal, of the 79th, also fell; and Lieutenants Oliphant, of the Goorkhas, and Battye, of the Guides, were wounded. A gallant private soldier of the 5th Goorkhas endeavoured to carry off Major Harding when he was wounded, and that officer was actually killed on the man's back.

Although a casual skirmish of this kind could have no decisive effect on the general position of affairs, it still, to a certain extent, encouraged the enemy; and as in the course of the next few days they received reinforcements to the amount of 3,000 men from the distant country of Bajour, they again showed signs of activity, and a determination to attack our right defences. These accordingly were reinforced; the Crag Picket was enlarged and strengthened, and defended by 160 men. It was also flanked by some mountain guns, placed on a plateau near its foot.

During the night of November 12th, the enemy pertinaciously assaulted the Crag, but, fortunately, they found Major Brownlow there ready to receive them. He describes the attack as follows:—

Before dark I had every man in his place for the night, with strict orders as to the nature of his duties, and the direction of his fire in case of attack. About 10 p.m. their watchfires showed us that the enemy were in movement, and descending in great numbers to the hollow in our front, which in half an hour was full of them. Their suppressed voices soon broke into yells of defiance, and they advanced in masses to our attack, their numbers being, so far as I could judge from sight and sound, at least 2,000. I allowed them to approach within a hundred yards, and then opened a rapid and well-sustained file-fire from our front, which I believe did great execution, and soon silenced their shouts, and drove them under cover—some to the broken and wooded ground to our left, and the rest to the ravine below us.

In half an hour they rallied, and, assembling in almost increased numbers, rushed to the attack—this time assaulting on our front, as well as on the left. They were received with the greatest steadiness, and again recoiled before our fire. These attacks continued until 4 a.m., each becoming weaker than the last, and many of them being mere feints to enable them to carry off their dead and wounded. During the night I received very valuable assistance from Captain Hughes's mountain battery. From his position about 250 yank below, and in the right rear, of the Crag, he made most successful practice, being guided, as to direction and range, by voice from our post. Before the attack commenced he pitched two shells into the watchfire of the enemy, which must have done considerable damage.

Notwithstanding the failure of the enemy in their night attack, their resolution to capture the Crag seemed undiminished, and the following morning they renewed their attempts, and for a time met with success. Lieutenant Davidson, of the 1st Punjab Infantry, was in command of the picket, when by a sudden assault the enemy succeeded in overpowering his party, and took possession of the work. Lieutenant Davidson, who behaved in a most heroic manner, was killed at his post. The loss of this outwork was a most serious matter. The approach to it was so steep and rocky, that its recapture, with a determined enemy flushed with success on its summit, was very difficult.

It so completely overlooked the other defences, that the ground below was almost untenable, and, to add to the general confusion, the camp-followers with their animals began to fly. Major Keyes, Major Ross, Captain Hughes, and other officers on the spot, endeavoured, by collecting what men were at hand, to stem the tide of retreat, and to present a bold front. It was a critical moment.

General Chamberlain writes:—

I was in the camp below when the Crag Picket fell into the hands of the enemy, and my attention having been accidentally drawn to the unusual dust and confusion caused by the rush of camp-followers and animals down the hill, I felt convinced that some reverse had occurred, and immediately sent forward Her Majesty's 101st Royal Bengal Fusiliers, which was fortunately under arms for another purpose.

Lieutenant-Colonel Salusbury commanded the regiment, and his orders were to push up the hill as fast as practicable, and to retake the Crag at any cost, and he was quite the man to carry them out. The ascent was long and steep, but the regiment, with their colonel at their head, never halted, and, in spite of all difficulties, in five-and-twenty minutes stood victorious on the crest of the work. Thus for the second time this key of the position was recovered.

For the next few days there was another short cessation of the violent attacks of the enemy, during which time General Chamberlain effected an important change in the disposition of his force; and it may therefore be useful to recapitulate briefly the previous events, and to explain the reasons of his present decision. It has already been pointed out, that the position originally taken up in the Umbeylah Pass was intended to have been temporary, and that our prolonged halt was due to unforeseen causes; and the general was therefore compelled to make the best of it. It has also been shown, that its chief weakness consisted in the isolation of its flanks, the retention of which, however, was of vital necessity so long as the main body remained below.

During the three weeks of our stay, the confederate tribes had received large reinforcements, and, having also discovered our weak points, they by incessant attacks not only inflicted great loss upon us, but almost wore out the troops; and on two occasions they temporarily gained possession of the Crag Picket, and were able to boast of other trivial successes. As some delay must occur before sufficient reserves could arrive to enable General Chamberlain to act on the offensive, he therefore, with a view of strengthening his position,[1] determined on abandoning altogether the pickets on the Gooroo Mountain, and on concentrating his force on the ground already held on the slope of the Mahabun.

In short, he drew back his left flank, and concentrated his force on his right. There can be no doubt but that, in a military point of view, this was a judicious arrangement. Instead of holding a series of straggling posts, perched up on rocks on two separate mountains, with his main body down in a hollow gorge, he would now have his troops well in hand, the different works could be reinforced with comparative ease, and only one vital point (the Crag) remained to be defended.

It is true that, by relinquishing the Gooroo Mountain, he also gave up the route by the Umbeylah Pass to Eusofzye; but it was never a safe or a good one, and the new road (which had been already completed) to the plains rendered the loss of the pass immaterial. In anticipation of the intended move, the commissariat stores, the reserve ammunition, &c., were carefully carried up to the right, and then, all being ready, the movement itself was finally carried out during the night of November 17. The vigilance of the enemy had failed them for once, and when daylight broke on the 18th, to their astonishment the 'Eagle's Nest' and all the pickets on the Gooroo Mountain were silent and empty.

---

1. Refer to the Frontispiece.

Exasperated probably by the success of our manoeuvre, or imagining that it was the precursor of a general retreat, the enemy rushed into the abandoned gorge in great numbers, flaunting their standards; and swarming up the ridges in front of our new position, before the troops were well settled in their places, commenced an attack on some small advanced breastworks, which were held by 140 men of the Ferozepore Regiment, under Major Ross. Our men, overpowered by numbers, at first gave way; but on being reinforced by two companies of the 71st Highlanders under Major Parker, a company of the 101st under Lieutenant Chapman, and some native troops, the posts were re taken.

The enemy, however, gradually increased in numbers, surrounded the breastworks, and forced our troops again to relinquish the ground, and to fall back on the main defences. Our losses on this occasion were very considerable, including several distinguished young officers—namely, Captain C. Smith, 71st; Lieutenant T. S. Jones, of the 79th Highlanders (a volunteer); Lieutenant W. F. Moseley, of the Ferozepore Regiment; and Lieutenant Chapman, the adjutant of the 101st. Of the last it is related that, when lying in the outwork, feeling his wound to be mortal, he begged his men to leave him, and to assist Captain Smith instead.

CHAPTER 11

The Enemy Again Assault and Capture the Crag Picket

The confederate tribes, consisting of the Fanatics; the men of the Mahabun; of Bonair, Swat, Bajour, and other secluded valleys, joined by a sprinkling of men from our own border villages, were now in such force that the hill-sides literally swarmed with them; and although they had hitherto been foiled in their attempts to capture our position, they resolved on one more desperate effort, and for the third time selected the Crag Picket as the point of attack.

All these great assaults of the enemy were carried out on the same simple and uniform plan. Taking up a position under cover within short range, and overlooking the work to be assaulted, with only the muzzles of their matchlocks appearing above the sheltering rocks, they would open as heavy a fire as their means permitted, and thus force our men to lie close behind their breastworks. The bolder spirits of the mountaineers—men armed with short swords, and who had fully made up their minds to a hand-to-hand fight—then advancing rapidly and with great courage to the very foot of the work, and collecting under cover of the rocks, would pause for awhile to regain their breath, and to prepare for a final rush; so that sometimes, almost before our men were aware of their immediate vicinity, showers of stones falling inside the work would be the first intimation that the enemy were close at hand. The mountaineers did not even hesitate to bring forward large standards, and to elevate them tauntingly within a few yards of the breastwork.

In opposition to their bold attitude of vigorous defiance, we could only offer that of dogged resistance; and defensive warfare of this kind, when prolonged, is always rather discouraging. Men who have been compelled for days and nights together, to be in crowded masses behind stone walls, waiting for enemies who may choose their own moment for attack, and are sure to come in force, inevitably become dispirited. The prolonged uncertainty preys upon their thoughts, and the inaction cools their blood. Our soldiers, far better armed than the mountaineers, and having all the advantages of discipline and good leaders, still found their superiority thus in great measure neutralised.

In the open, the issue of a fight, even with numbers against them, could never be doubtful for a moment; and it was almost a natural impulse among our men to jump from their cover, and bring the matter to an immediate issue; but the general safety of the whole position would not admit of this exceptional course, as our numbers were as yet insufficient to enable us to take the offensive. Day after day, therefore, our soldiers had to submit to this disadvantageous warfare, and its dispiriting effects were already becoming palpable. General Chamberlain, after the loss of his pickets on November 18, had felt compelled to telegraph as follows:—

> The troops have now been hard-worked both day and night for a month, and having to meet fresh enemies with loss is telling. We much need reinforcements. I find it difficult to meet the enemy's attacks, and provide convoys for supplies and wounded sent to the rear. If you can give some fresh corps to relieve those most reduced in numbers and dash, the relieved corps can be sent to the plains and used in support. This is urgent.

On the morning of November 20, the enemy showed in great numbers on the high ground overlooking the Crag Picket, which was held by a hundred men of the 101st Fusiliers, and a hundred men of the 20th Punjab Infantry. The attack continued for hours, and the men of the tribes gradually advanced to within a few feet of the breastworks, and displayed numerous standards. Suddenly, about 3 o'clock in the afternoon (owing, as General Chamberlain says, to the unaccountable conduct of a portion of the garrison), the enemy gained possession of the crest.

The defences of the picket were in two parts; but although the upper had thus fallen, the officers and men in the lower held on gallantly until the place became quite untenable, more than two-thirds of them being killed or wounded. Major Delafosse, of the 101st, and Captain Rogers, of the 20th, distinguished themselves by their courage; as also Ensign A. E. Sanderson and Assistant-Surgeon Pile, of the 101st. The two latter were, unfortunately, killed whilst endeavouring to rally their men.

Thus for the third time had this commanding outwork fallen. Flushed with their success, the enemy swarmed into the abandoned breastworks, capturing some muskets and boxes of ammunition; and shouts of triumph rose from the hill-sides all round, as the tribes beheld our men retreating down the rocks. Victory, however, was, soon snatched from their eager grasp. The 71st Highland Light Infantry, who had taken a full share in every action of the campaign, were the men selected by Chamberlain to retrieve the fortunes of the day, and they were not wanting in this hour of need.

Although every credit must be given to our native regiments, and although the officers employed with them had shown high qualities as leaders, still it must be remembered, after all, that the quarrel which was being fought out on the Mahabun was an English one, and it was therefore fitting that English regiments should be relied on in the last resort. Such has been, and ever must be, the case in India. Devoted and brave as are many of the native soldiery, they have not the feelings, nor can they be imbued with the same sympathies, which tie the English soldiers to their officers; so that in critical moments the latter can alone be fully depended on, whether it be to assault or to defend a desperate position.

General Chamberlain therefore sent for the 71st Highlanders, and associating with them the brave little Goorkhas, prepared once more to storm the Crag. In the meantime the field and mountain guns, which were in position at various points of our general line of defence, were turned in the direction of the captured work; and by an incessant flight of shells, they held the mountaineers in check, prevented them from following up their advantage, and forced them to lie close under cover of the rocks on the summit.

Under a perfect storm of matchlock-balls and showers of rocks hurled from the top, Colonel Hope, the gallant leader of the Highlanders, deliberately formed his men at the foot of the Crag; and sending the Goorkhas to turn the flank, he placed himself at the head of his corps, and with a cool determination, which excited the admiration not only of his own men, but of every soldier in the force, proceeded to march up the height. The mountaineers throughout the war had shown themselves ready to do and to dare a great deal, but they were not quite prepared for the direct assault of a Highland regiment, which in open day, with its colonel at its head, was steadily climbing the steep ascent, and which would infallibly in a few seconds close upon them, with a volley and a bayonet-charge.

The storm of shells which had been raining for the preceding half-hour, and shattering the rocks and trees on the summit, had somewhat shaken their confidence, which was completed by the rapid approach of Colonel Hope and his men. The mountaineers evacuated the works almost as the Highlanders reached them, and our troops then pursued and drove them off along the ridges. General Chamberlain, ever foremost in danger, having felt it his duty to accompany the troops in so critical an attack, was, unfortunately, severely wounded in the arm, and Colonel Hope also was dangerously wounded in the thigh. Our lost ground was thus recovered, but at the cost of two distinguished men, the first and second in command of the force, and who were rendered unable again to take part in the war.

The tables on the following pages, showing the number of casualties at each great attack, and nominal lists of the officers killed and wounded, will be of interest:—

RETURN SHOWING THE NUMBERS KILLED AND WOUNDED AT EACH ATTACK.

Date.	Name of Attack.	Killed.			Wounded.			Total.	Remarks.
		English Officers.	Native Officers.	Men.	English Officers.	Native Officers.	Men.		
Oct. 26	Attack on the Eagle's Nest.	2	1	28	2	9	87	129	
Oct. 30	Recapture of the Crag Picket (first time)	,,	1	12	2	2	36	53	
Nov. 6	Attack on Major Harding's party	3	1	34	2	2	37	79	
Nov. 13	Recapture of the Crag Picket (second time)	1	1	49	1	3	104	159	
Nov. 18	Attack on our change of position	4	,,	40	1	,,	74	119	
Nov. 20	Recapture of the Crag Picket (third time)	2	,,	25	5	1	104	137	
,,	Other minor attacks	2	,,	25	2	,,	26	55	
	Total	14	4	213	15	17	468	731	

NOMINAL LIST OF OFFICERS KILLED.

Date.	Rank and Name.	Regiment.	
Oct. 22	Lieutenant Gillies	Royal Artillery	
Nov. 6	Ensign C. B. Murray	71st Highland Light Infantry	
Nov. 18	Captain C. F. Smith		
Nov. 19	Captain R. B. Aldridge		
Nov. 6	Lieutenant Dougal	79th Highlanders	(Volunteers, doing duty with the 71st)
Nov. 18	Lieutenant Jones		
Nov. 18	Lieutenant H. H. Chapman	101st Royal Bengal Fusiliers	
Nov. 20	Ensign A. R. Sanderson		
„	Assistant-Surgeon W. Pile		
Nov. 18	Lieutenant J. P. Davidson	1st Punjab Infantry	
Oct. 26	Lieutenant Clifford	3rd Punjab Infantry	
Nov. 18	Lieutenant W. F. Moseley	14th Ferozepore Regt.	
Oct. 26	Lieutenant Richmond	20th Native Infantry	
Nov. 6	Major G. W. Harding	Bombey Staff Corps	

NOMINAL LIST OF OFFICERS WOUNDED.

Date.	Rank and Name.	Regiment.	Remarks.
Nov. 20	Brigadier-General Sir Neville Chamberlain, K.C.B.	Staff	
Nov. 20	Lieutenant Anderson	„	
Oct. 22	Lieutenant Brown	Royal Engineers	
Nov. 20	Colonel W. Hope, C.B.	71st Highland Lt. Infantry	
Nov. 13	Ensign C. M. Stockley	101st Royal Bengal Fusiliers	
Oct. 30	Major C. P. Keyes	1st Punjab Regiment	Wounded twice
Oct. 30 / Nov. 6	Lieutenant H. W. Pitcher	1st Punjab Regiment	
Nov. 6	Lieutenant J. G. Oliphant	5th Goorkhas	
Nov. 20	Major J. P. Campbell	5th Goorkhas	
Nov. 20	Lieut.-Colonel J. L. Vaughan	5th Punjab Regiment	
Nov. 6	Lieutenant W. Battye	Guide Infantry	
Nov. 13	Lieutenant A. D. C. Inglis	Ferozepore Regiment	
Oct. 26	Lieutenant F. Drake	32nd Native Infantry	
Oct. 26	Lieutenant Barron	Survey Department	

CHAPTER 12

Summary of the Military and Political Aspects of the War

The attack of November 20 proved to be the last attempt made by the enemy to drive us from our position on the Mahabun. There was a considerable lull; and when offensive operations were renewed, it became our turn to take the initiative. Could the confederate tribes, however, have divined the moral effect which they had already produced at Lahore, it is probable they would have been tempted to strike hard once more for victory. But, disheartened by repeated failures, and growing rather weary of the war, they waited for distant reinforcements before renewing their efforts; and in truth, in some of these respects, our condition and theirs was very similar.

The aspect of affairs was certainly grave. The enemy, although they had not succeeded in driving us out of the mountains, had, at all events, forced us to halt and entrench at the end of the first day's march; and they had hitherto entirely prevented our fulfilling the objects of the expedition. Our losses in action had been considerable, and our soldiers were falling sick from constant exposure, night-watches, and overwork. Reinforcements were hurrying up, but were still at a distance. It need not be inferred that there was any imminent danger of a catastrophe, nor could the utmost efforts of all the tribes of Central Asia, perhaps, effect much against the power of England in the East, if really put forth; but the mere expense which was being incurred was out of all proportion to the original objects of the expedition.

If the military situation was serious, the political one was, perhaps, even less promising. Our march beyond the border had not only roused and exasperated the tribes in the immediate neighbourhood, but the frontier, it may almost be said, for hundreds of miles was in commotion. Even at Cabool there was sympathy for, if not a promise of active support to, the tribes. Within our own territories the contagion was spreading: there were wounded men lying in the villages, who were known to have been up in the mountains fighting against us. And there was another danger, perhaps, even greater than all.

Faithful and courageous as our native frontier regiments had as yet proved themselves, still it was contrary to human nature to suppose that they could go on, week after week, fighting against their kith and kin, suffering severe losses, and yet, so far as their limited means enabled them to judge, without much prospect of ultimate success. The ties of discipline had not yet given way, but there must be a limit to the faithful endurance of aliens and mercenaries. The late Major Hugh James, C.B., an officer of great ability and matured experience in frontier policy, who had arrived from England at this crisis, and had just joined the force as Civil Commissioner, reported in very explicit terms. He wrote:—

> Meanwhile the excitement was spreading far and wide. The Momunds on the Peshawur border were beginning to make hostile demonstrations at Shubkudder,[1] for the first time since their signal defeat near the same place, in 1852, by the late Lord Clyde. Rumours were also reaching me from Kohat of expected raids by the Wuzeerees and Othman-Khail. Emissaries from Cabool and Jellalabad were with the Akhoond, who had been also further reinforced by Ghuzzun Khan, the chief of Dher, and 6,000 men. On December 5 the Momunds made a raid into our territories at Shubkudder, in repelling which Lieutenant

---

1. A small outpost in the Peshawur valley, at the foot of the mountains.

Bishop was killed.

Major James added that it was truly a formidable and dangerous combination, and that immediate action was necessary, to save the Government from a war, which would inevitably lead to the most serious complications, involving us not only with all the tribes on our border, and many of our own subjects both in Peshawur and Kohat, but also, in all probability, with Afghanistan.

The Lieutenant-Governor of the Punjab had, doubtless, long and anxiously considered the untoward aspect of affairs; and at length, when the telegrams from Sir Neville Chamberlain arrived, announcing the severe actions of November 18 and 20, he looked upon the matter as so serious that he was actually prepared to advocate the immediate withdrawal of the whole force to the plains, and the abandonment of the expedition.

The report of the Lahore Government on the war says:—

General Chamberlain's telegram of the 19th showed a state of things which gave rise to serious apprehensions, in the mind of the Lieutenant-Governor, concerning the position of the force during the days which must elapse before the brigade could reach it.

The report goes on to say that the Lieutenant-Governor, considering the delay which must occur before reinforcements could arrive, and the disadvantages which the force would suffer from constant exposure to repeated attacks, which it could not meet on the offensive, and that any disaster would be a great political misfortune, was of opinion that, under all the circumstances, the force ought to be withdrawn to the plains. The Lieutenant-Governor, further considering that the general-officer on the spot should be free to act solely according to the military necessities of the case, without regard to political considerations, and believing that, in the event of retirement, General Chamberlain's moral position would be fortified by the sanction of the local Government, did not hesitate to take the responsibility on himself, and telegraphed to Major James accordingly.

General Chamberlain was lying in a small tent on the mountain, seriously wounded, weak in body but undaunted in spirit, when the message was brought to him. Major James writes:—

On the 21st I received His Honour's telegram of the previous day, authorising the withdrawal of the force to Permouli,[2] should General Chamberlain consider it desirable on military grounds. The General was at the time suffering from his wound, and unable to discuss the question in detail; but he signified his opinion that such a step would be most unadvisable.

Major James himself also at once pointed out to the Government the calamitous effects which, he felt assured, would ensue from a withdrawal at that time, both on the border and in our districts, and the protracted campaign to which it would necessarily commit us. The civil and military authorities on the spot were plainly of opinion that no withdrawal should take place.

It is quite clear that the Lieutenant-Governor at Lahore anticipated a disaster, and he evidently acted under the impression that the chief responsibility of a war beyond the frontier, in which several thousands of the British Army were engaged, rested on his shoulders. Indeed, the last paragraph of his report, already alluded to, reverts to the subject, and says:—

During the events which have been reported, the Lieutenant-Governor was placed in a position of unusual difficulty. The Governor-General, Lord Elgin, was in a dying state in the interior of the hills, cut off from telegraphic communication, and unable to transact business. His Honour was therefore obliged to act solely according to his own judgment. His great object, in accordance with the declared policy of the Government, was to prevent the extension of military operations in the hills, and to bring the campaign to a rapid conclusion.

It certainly was an unfortunate circumstance that at so criti-

2. A small village in the plains of Eusofzye.

cal a period, the viceroy, Lord Elgin, should have been struck down, and his Lordship was then at the point of death in the Himalayas; still, in other respects, the Lieutenant-Governor was by no means without support. Sir Hugh Rose, the Commander-in-Chief in India, and a member of the Supreme Government, had left Lord Elgin's bedside, and had arrived in all haste at Lahore on November 14; and therefore, at the very moment that the Lieutenant-Governor was contemplating withdrawal, and telegraphing instructions to that effect, he had ample means of ascertaining on the spot, the opinions, and of being guided by the judgment, of the highest military authority in the country.

What Sir Hugh Rose thought of the proposition is plain enough. In the first place, he wrote to the other members of the Government at Calcutta, remonstrating against the proposed withdrawal, pointing out the danger of such a policy, and the loss of prestige which would necessarily follow. In the next, he ordered large reinforcements to proceed by forced marches to the frontier, so that the great northern road from Lahore to Peshawur, during the last days of November, was crowded with cavalry, artillery, and infantry, all hurrying upwards. At the beginning of December there were five-and-twenty thousand men north of the Jhelum!

Lord Elgin died on November 20. His successor, Sir William Denison, reached Calcutta from Madras on December 2, and on his arrival found that the majority of the Council were in favour of withdrawing the troops, and had even issued orders to that effect. Sir William, however, induced the members of the Government to reconsider and, ultimately, to cancel their first decision. In a clear and able minute on the subject, he first of all gives a summary of the events of the campaign, and of the urgent reasons put forward by the Lieutenant-Governor of the Punjab in favour of withdrawal; and the minute then continues as follows:—

The Government, yielding to these pressing instances, conceded to the wish of the Lieutenant-Governor, and gave directions, on November 26, that the troops should be withdrawn as soon as it could be done without risk of military disaster, or without seriously compromising our military reputation.

While, however, these messages were moving backwards and forwards, events were progressing. The troops at the head of the pass maintained their position, causing serious loss to the enemy, who were consequently getting disheartened; reinforcements were moving up; the troops which were intended to form the camp at Lahore were rapidly approaching the scene of action; better means of conveyance for stores and ammunition had been provided. The threat of snow proved to be a delusion, and the fears of the Lieutenant-Governor of the Punjab, that risings would take place in consequence of the removal of troops to the frontier, were seen to be groundless.

Such was the state of things when I landed at Calcutta, and such being the case, I felt myself compelled to ask the Council to modify the instructions previously given for the withdrawal of the troops. . . .

It has been assumed, somewhat gratuitously, that the operation, as originally schemed out, was quite simple and easy, involving only a march through a rough district, to which little or no resistance would be offered; and the blame of the failure of the plan has been, in my opinion, most improperly and unfairly thrown upon General Chamberlain. I mention these circumstances merely for the purpose of expressing my opinion, that they have been improperly imported into the discussion.

What the Government had to consider was the simple fact that a body of troops ordered—whether wisely or not is nothing to the purpose—into a district for a specific purpose had been resisted, and prevented from executing that purpose; had sustained some loss, but were now in a position to overcome all resistance, and to carry out the spirit of the original instructions, and very probably the letter; and that, under a different and much more unfavourable state of things, it had been induced to order a retrograde movement of the troops, which order it was requested to reconsider.

My opinion was, and is, that the withdrawal of the troops from what has proved to be merely a defensive position, would be considered by the mountain tribes as equivalent to a victory; and although I did not doubt the possibility of withdrawing the force without serious loss, I yet felt convinced that the moral effect of such a move upon our troops would be of the worst description. I was and am of opinion that a movement in retreat would probably bring about all the financial difficulties so vividly described by Sir Charles Trevelyan; for the certain result would be such a series of aggressions on the part of the mountain tribes, elated by their supposed success in causing us to retreat, as would compel us to make a more serious attack upon them in the course of next year, for the purpose of asserting our superiority.

The idea of withdrawal having been thus abandoned, the viceroy at once telegraphed to Lahore, expressing his entire confidence in the measures of the commander-in-chief, and desired that the military operations might be continued with vigour. The result was (as will be seen), that as soon as sufficient reinforcements reached the mountain, General Garvock, who had succeeded Chamberlain in the command, issued from his entrenchments; and at daylight, on December 15, met the enemy in great strength on the crest of the mountain above Laloo, and struck them a blow which sent them staggering back into the Chumla valley: following them up, he again defeated them at the foot of the Bonair hills, in the presence of the assembled thousands of the confederate tribes, and the war collapsed at once.

Sir William Denison remained but a few weeks as Viceroy, but he had the satisfaction of feeling that a most dangerous state of affairs was brought to a speedy conclusion by his good sense and determination, backed up by the vigour of Sir Hugh Rose, and the valour of the troops engaged.

CHAPTER 13

Termination of the War

During the last days of November and the early part of December, the war, so far as active operations were concerned, rather languished. The enemy swarmed in the mountains, infested the communications, and threatened attack; but although Ghuzzun Khan, with 6,000 men from the distant province of Dher, had joined the Akhoond's standard, they still hesitated to precipitate themselves against entrenchments which had been strengthened, and which were vigilantly guarded, the upper ones by English soldiers. Meanwhile our reinforcements were at hand, and Major James, employing the interval in negotiations, induced some few hill-chiefs of minor note to return to their homes.

The Bonairs, indeed, were half inclined for peace. They had borne the brunt of the campaign, and had lost many men, and they now found their valley overrun, and their limited supplies eaten up, by crowds of hungry mountaineers from distant provinces. The last comers, living at free quarters, and not having yet felt the weight of our arm, were, however, still full of enthusiasm: so that, although in numbers the confederate tribes were stronger than ever, a certain want of unanimity was arising in their councils.

On the other hand, our force was steadily on the increase. The 7th Fusiliers, the 93rd Highlanders, and several native corps arrived; consequently General Garvock, who came from Peshawur and assumed the command, found himself at the head of nearly 9,000 men, all eager for the fray.

On December 10, the chiefs of Bonair arrived in camp, to discuss terms of peace with the Commissioner, and left again the following day, agreeing on their part to accompany the British troops to the destruction of Mulka and to the expulsion of the Hindostanees. They, however, intimated that these proposals, mild as they were, might not receive the approval of the *Akhoond* and other influential men of the tribes, and the event proved that their surmises were right. The failure of this attempted negotiation is hardly to be regretted.

Had peace been made before we had proved our power by an advance and a victory, it is not to be doubted but that we should have suffered in prestige. The mountaineers would, almost naturally, have concluded that after all our efforts we were only too glad to make terms and to leave the Mahabun. Besides which, our position during the last three weeks had much improved; and although it might not be necessary to exact stringent terms from our enemies, still, as they had combined and fought hard against us, and, further, as a great expense had been incurred, it seemed desirable at all events that we should improve the opportunity by showing them that our power was completely in the ascendant, and their country at our mercy.

During the three days subsequent to the departure of the Bonair chiefs, the enemy made a vast display of strength in the Chumla valley and neighbouring hills. Standards might be counted by the dozen, and the watchfires at night betokened the presence of many thousands. Late in the afternoon of December 14, a solitary messenger arrived in camp, with information that the Bonairs were still willing to make peace, but that the *Akhoond* and others refused compliance with our terms. This was significant, and portended immediate attack; but General Garvock, who with his troops had been chafing at the delay, was prepared for the emergency, and anticipated their movements by one of his own. His force had been divided into two brigades — the one under Lieutenant-Colonel Wilde, C.B., of the Guides; the other under Colonel W. W. Turner, C.B., of the 97th Regiment. Leaving 3,000 men to take care of his entrenchments, at daylight on December 15, the general led his two brigades out along the ridge of the mountain, and soon came upon the enemy.

About two miles beyond the Crag Picket stood the small village of Laloo, and a few hundred yards in front of it, one of the great spurs running up from the Chumla valley terminated in a lofty peak dominating the whole ridge. On this natural stronghold the men of the tribes had established themselves in great force, flying their standards over the mountain-top, and prepared to abide the last issues of war. They had increased the ordinary difficulties of the ascent by occasional breastworks, so that it was a most formidable position to take by assault. Our skirmishers, who had easily driven in the outlying mountaineers, then halted about 600 yards in front of, and looking up at, the conical peak, and, supported by the mountain-guns, waited for the arrival of the main body of the two brigades.

These mountain batteries, just referred to, proved most useful auxiliaries during the war. Their light ordnance, carriages, and ammunition being all carried on mule-back, they are thus quite independent of roads, and are able to accompany infantry over any ground, however rough, and to come into action on the most restricted space. It only seems a pity that the rare and valuable experience thus gained in hill-warfare should be limited to native soldiers, the men of these batteries being recruited on the spot, like the rest of the Punjab Force. The several regiments of the two brigades, as they came up, were formed under shelter of the broken ground, Colonel Turner's brigade being on the right; and when all was ready, General Garvock directed 'the advance' to be sounded from the centre of the line.

At that signal 5,000 men rose up from their cover, and, with loud cheers and volleys of musketry, rushed to the assault—the regiments of Pathans, Sikhs, and Goorkhas all vying with the English soldiers as to who should first reach the enemy. From behind every rock and shrub, at the foot of the conical peak small parties of mountaineers jumped up, and fled as the advancing columns approached them. It took but a few seconds to cross the open ground, and then the steep ascent began; our men having to climb from rock to rock, and their regular formation necessarily becoming much broken.

Foremost among the many could be distinguished the scarlet uniforms of the 101st Fusiliers, which, led by Colonel Salusbury and Major Lambert, steadily breasted the mountain, and captured the defences in succession at the point of the bayonet, the enemy's standards dropping as their outworks fell; whilst here and there the prostrate figures of soldiers, scattered about the rocks, proved that the hill-men were striking hard to the last. Nothing, however, could withstand the impetuosity of the assault; and although many of the enemy stood their ground bravely, and fell at their posts, their gallantry was of no avail; and ere many minutes had elapsed, the peak from foot to summit was in the possession of British soldiers.

This direct assault had been accomplished chiefly by the regiments of Colonel Wilde's brigade; and in the meantime Colonel Turner, with the 7th Fusiliers and other corps, passing round by the right of the position, turned it and, moving rapidly on, captured the village of Laloo. The mountaineers then fled, thousands of them passing down the steep glades, through the pine forests leading to the Chumla valley, many hundred feet below.

The rapidity and vigour of General Garvock's movements had, indeed, utterly disconcerted the plans of the tribes. Accustomed hitherto to assemble at their leisure, and to choose their own time for attack, they had been following out the same course on the present occasion; and during the previous night large bodies of them had evidently been collecting at various points for a general assault; so that whilst General Garvock was driving great masses before him down the ridges below Laloo, others, ignorant of the catastrophe, were climbing up from the Umbeylah Pass, and attacking our entrenched camp, where, however, they found all ready to receive them, and were vigorously repulsed.

This was the first general defeat the enemy had experienced, and they were not left long to recover from its effects. At day-light the following morning, the British troops were again in movement, one brigade (Colonel Wilde's) marching down direct on Umbeylah, accompanied by a regiment of light cavalry, 400 strong, under Colonel Probyn, which had been brought up from Eusofzye in anticipation of a fight in the valley. The troopers led their horses with difficulty down the steep mountainside, and then mounted at the foot in readiness for an attack. In the meantime Colonel Turner's brigade had made a detour by Laloo, and after a tedious march reached the Chumla valley and deployed.

The enemy were drawn up on a minor ridge in front of Umbeylah, and at first showed a determination to try the issue of another battle; but with one brigade in their front, another coming down on their flank, and with cavalry eager to charge them in the open, they prudently but sulkily fell back, skirting along the edge of the hills under cover of the broken ground. Late in the afternoon Colonel Turner, with a portion of his brigade, consisting of two Sikh Pioneer corps in line, and a wing of the 7th Fusiliers in support, swept across the valley; and passing Umbeylah, advanced towards the hills which divide the Chumla from Bonair—many thousands of the enemy looking down and watching his movements from the slopes and crests above.

Hardly had the regiments arrived within a few hundred yards of the base of the hills, than the mountaineers opened a heavy matchlock-fire; and suddenly, from the broken ground and ravines, several hundreds of them, who had been lying concealed, rushed out sword in hand, furiously attacked the Pioneers, penetrated their ranks, and for a moment staggered them; but, rallied by their officers, and supported by the Fusiliers, the two regiments quickly turned again on their assailants, of whom hardly a man ultimately escaped. Although this sharp attack had only lasted a few minutes, the enemy had found time to single out the English officers; Lieutenant Alexander being killed, and Major Wheler, Captain Chamberlain, Lieutenants Nott and Marsh, wounded.

In the meantime three field-guns,[1] which had been brought down on elephants and horsed in the valley, shelled the crowded heights; and the mountaineers, thus finding themselves exposed to attack by every arm in succession, and that neither the hills nor the plains afforded them protection, quickly withdrew. The losses of the British in the two days' engagements amounted to 172 killed and wounded.

The effect of these actions was immediate and decisive. The men of Bajour and of Dher, who had come so far and were so eager for war, now tied to their native fastnesses. The *Akhoond* and his followers were no more to be seen; and the chiefs of Bonair, relieved from the presence of overbearing allies, gladly came into camp and agreed to terms of peace. The natural course would now have been to send a column at once to destroy Mulka, the original object of the expedition, and which was about twenty-five miles off; but the difficulties of quick movement, the anxiety to terminate the war and leave the mountains, led the Commissioner to agree with the Bonairs that they should destroy the village, a few officers, with an escort, alone proceeding with them to see it carried out. The defect of this arrangement was, that treachery, or even a sudden outbreak of fanaticism, might have led to serious complications.

Mulka proved to be a large handsome village, recently built of pinewood, standing high on a northern slope of the Mahabun, whose snowy crests rose precipitously behind it, whilst in its front a vast panorama of mountains stretched away as far as the eye could reach. The village contained numerous workshops and a rude powder-factory, but was found deserted. It was fired in the presence of the English officers on December 22, and the great column of smoke, as it rose from the ruins, proclaimed that the object of the Government had been at length accomplished, and that the Fanatics were houseless wanderers.

This final act of the war was witnessed by a crowd of moun-

---

1. Captain Griffin, the gallant and energetic officer who commanded these guns, was killed in the following year at the assault of Dalimkote, in Bootan. During the Crimean war he had served for several months in the batteries before Sebastopol.

taineers belonging to the minor tribes of the Mahabun, who gradually collected near the spot and angrily watched the conflagration. There was sorrow as well as anger in their hearts. In their villages were many fresh graves of relatives, who had fallen during the campaign; and what also deeply moved them, was the hated presence of Englishmen in a part of the country hitherto sacred from intrusion. As there seemed a possibility of their proceeding to acts of violence, they were addressed both by the Commissioner [2] and by an influential chief of Bonair; and at length they went away silently and sullenly to their homes, and the English officers with their escort marched back to the Chumla valley.

---

2. Colonel P. Taylor, C.B.

CHAPTER 14

The Advance of Russia in Asia

On Christmas Day the British troops left the mountains, and once more stood on the plains of Eusofzye, the mountaineers destroying the entrenchments, and breaking up the roads, as they marched away.

Thus ended the Frontier War of 1863. Intended at the outset as a mere excursion, to drive off a few fanatical robbers who had long infested the border, it speedily grew into a considerable war, the Mahomedan tribes, under the impression that their religion and country were in danger, combining against us. It is true that, in spite of all opposition, we accomplished our original object; but the anxiety, the expense, and the losses incurred, were out of all proportion to the end achieved, and our long detention perhaps rather injured our prestige. In the retrospect, therefore, the campaign is not altogether satisfactory, but the experience gained is valuable, and well worthy of careful consideration.

It seems clear that the tribes whose homes are in the long range of mountains forming our north-west border, although independent of each other, are still so bound by ties of religion, country, and race, that however desirous we may be, in the event of a quarrel with one section, to localise our operations, and however honest in refraining from conquest, our views will almost inevitably be misinterpreted, and, if time admit, a combination will be formed against us.

At all events, we must be prepared for such an event; and as the bravery of the mountaineers, the ruggedness of their country, and its scanty supplies, combine to render military operations on our part difficult, we should therefore endeavour to perfect our arrangements before we move; and it cannot be too constantly borne in mind, that efficient transport is one essential element of success. All troops on the frontier should be provided with mule-carriage, and officers and men be taught that quick movements involve personal self-denial and limited baggage.

Taking a general view of our position on this frontier, it certainly seems an insecure one—insecure not only from defective military organisation, but from its geographical features. We have crossed the Indus, and hold a narrow strip of flat country between the river and a chain of mountains; and our only defences are a few weakly-fortified posts, dotted here and there at long intervals, at the foot of the hills. We thus stand with a great river at our backs, and a vast aggregate of unruly mountaineers looking down upon us from strong commanding ground in our front. It is true that the tribes possess neither military organisation, nor the resources which would enable them to invade us with a view to conquest, as of old; but, secure in their native fastnesses, they can swoop down and plunder almost at will, whilst their punishment, as we have seen, is difficult.

Our long weak line of frontier is guarded, as already described, by troops raised upon the spot, who are not under the commander-in-chief, and, with the exception of Peshawur, there are no English soldiers to be seen. The impolicy of the divided command has long been notorious. Even as long ago as 1850, the anomaly was proposed to be abolished; but the personal differences between Lord Dalhousie, the Governor-General, and the then commander-in-chief, Sir Charles Napier, led to the adjournment of the question, which has remained in abeyance ever since.

One argument used by those who advocate the exclusive employment of native soldiers on the border, is that their wants are fewer, and that the climate is better suited to their constitutions. These, however, are hardly sound conclusions. The climate Trans-Indus, even in the hot season, is no worse than that of many stations garrisoned by English soldiers in the plains, and for several months in the cold weather it is delightful; and once in the hills, unless Englishmen have lost their pristine manly virtues, they are surely able to compete with natives, even though the marches be arduous and the fare somewhat scanty. If, even in the scorching plains, the personal vigour of our race has always been pre-eminent, now that we have a prospect of campaigning in a mountainous tract, the superiority ought to prove still more apparent.

The north-west frontier is at present the post of danger and of honour in India; the battles to be fought there are English ones; and therefore it is quite fitting that English soldiers should stand in the front line; and it appears to be a dangerous policy to allow local native levies to usurp their places.

Hitherto our professed object has been to maintain an armed neutrality all along this exposed border, and to resort to aggressive measures only in exceptional cases of serious misconduct on the part of our neighbours; but, in reality, the exceptions have almost become the rule. During the thirteen years from 1850 to 1863, no less than twenty expeditions have been sent into the mountains, and the numbers employed on each occasion are gradually increasing. It is no doubt feasible, by improved arrangements, to establish a more rigid military cordon, and thus to check incursions into our districts; but may it not be possible to achieve a far more complete and satisfactory result by an entire change of policy?

Instead of standing for ever sternly on our guard—holding the tribes, as it were, at arm's length, which has hitherto been the system of the Punjab Government—might we not hope by kindness and conciliation, by active friendship in short, to change the feelings of the mountaineers, so that they and their rugged country might become a bulwark, instead of, as at present, a perpetual menace? Powerful as we are, and possessed of boundless resources of all kinds, it is absurd to suppose that we could not gain the confidence and even the warm friendship of our needy neighbours, if we seriously desire to do so. Important events are now taking place in Afghanistan and still farther away in Central Asia, and therefore the day may not be distant when the possession of a strong frontier will be of great value to our dominion in the East.

In the early part of this account some extracts were given from the report of Mr. Temple, the former Secretary of the Lahore Government, on the frontier tribes; and it will be interesting now to make a further quotation, because, although written a few years back, it affords a clear account of the policy which has been pursued, and which is in force to this very day.

Mr. Temple says:—

The British Government has indeed organised an excellent defensive system; it has built or fitted up no less than fifteen forts, and fifty posts of various kinds, on this frontier; it has caused many hundreds of miles to be patrolled. But the unvarying experience of six years has proved that success cannot thus be attained, though doubtless the mode of defence is good and useful in its way. The independent hills are in the closest proximity to the line of defence; however well the posts may be placed, there will be villages and cultivation in front of them—that is, between them and the hills; everywhere there is inhabited territory within easy reach of the enemy; in many places our subjects live within a mile or two of their tormentors.

Under these circumstances, what human vigilance and arrangement can avail to entirely prevent the hill-men plundering in the valleys and the plains, and then escaping to their fastnesses with impunity? The assailants may often be foiled, but they will often succeed. To thoroughly prevent the hill-people by this method alone, it would require nothing less than a Chinese wall, securely manned, for 800 miles. But, in fact, the fears of these people must be worked upon; the root of the deeply-seated evil must be reached, and the headquarters of the offending tribe must be attacked in the hills.

They have already desisted partially, from the fear of these expeditions; if they were to become relieved of that apprehension, they would begin to harass and plunder again worse than ever. . . . . In fine, the whole argument terminates in this, that if expeditions were not resorted to, then all the territory within a night's run from the hills would virtually be given over to devastation.

If the latter event were to happen, and if the Government were not to be willing to chastise the hill-tribes, then our own Trans-Indus subjects would lose confidence, and would cease to be loyal, while the enemy gained heart. There would be some general combination against us, and sooner or later we should evacuate the Trans-Indus territory and the right bank of the Indus. If the right bank were lost, then the river itself would pass from our control; and then, with the loss of the Indus, there would be a sacrifice of advantages, political, physical, commercial, and moral, which it is not in the scope of this paper to describe.

But, in fact, the British Government has every encouragement to maintain its position beyond the Indus; for situated as it is, the representative of civilised strength in the midst of tribes which are rude and savage at present, but possess the elements of good and are susceptible of moral impressions, it has under Providence a noble mission to fulfil, and a purpose of regeneration to accomplish.

Mr. Temple, it will be seen, is a decided advocate of physical force; although at the same time he admits its partial failure, and is forced to the conclusion that real security can only be found in a well-manned wall 800 miles long!

Sir Charles Wood was the Secretary of State for India when the Sitana war took place; and early in 1864, summing up the events of the campaign, in a despatch to the Viceroy of India, he lays down the general principles which should guide our frontier policy, and which if carried out would doubtless have a conciliatory effect on the border-tribes.

He says:—

It is one of the conditions of our advanced frontier—bordering on mountain districts inhabited by needy and warlike tribes, proud of their independence, and from the earliest ages prone to habits of rapine and plunder,—that, from time to time, outrages should be committed upon our subjects and territories. The usual evils of this state of affairs are aggravated, in the district which has been the scene of these operations, by the presence of a body of Hindostanee and other Mahomedan fanatics, animated by a spirit of the most violent religious enthusiasm, and by hatred of the British rule.

Her Majesty's Government fully recognise the duty of making every exertion to check these outrages, and of affording every protection to the people under British sway. Individuals or tribes who injure our subjects, or make inroads on our districts, must be summarily and severely punished. But, for this purpose, it is not necessary to undertake distant and costly expeditions into mountain fastnesses, difficult of access, deficient in supplies, and offering every sort of objects to the advance of disciplined troops. Although our ability to penetrate the hills, and to engage successfully in hostile operations with these warlike tribes on their own ground, has been abundantly demonstrated, nevertheless, in such operations, we are placed at every disadvantage. The natives of the country, used to mountain warfare, and thoroughly acquainted with the localities, are able to advance or retreat at their pleasure, and to paralyse for a time the movements of disciplined soldiers. In the plains, on the contrary, where our cavalry and guns can be brought into action, we are perfectly irresistible.

The tribes, as a general rule, are badly armed, and unprovided with munitions of war. They have little coherence amongst themselves, except on special occasions, for a brief period, in defence of their own fastnesses, or under the influence of strong fanatical excitement. It is very difficult for them to assemble in any considerable numbers beyond their own frontiers. No force that they could collect and bring down from the mountains could stand against British troops, with cavalry and artillery; and it would be an easy matter to inflict heavy loss upon them, and drive them back to the hills.

There are, no doubt, cases in which it may be requisite that lightly-equipped and well-selected detachments should penetrate for short distances into the hills, and destroy the towns, rendezvous, and places of assembly of the offending tribes. Her Majesty's Government, however, desire to impress upon your Excellency, that an aggressive policy is wholly opposed to their wishes, as being contrary to the true interests of the State. If successful, it can only be for a time; we cannot hold these mountain districts, except at a ruinous cost of valuable lives and money.

When we withdraw, the inhabitants are sure to resume their former habits, doubly embittered against us by the recollection of the injuries which they have sustained at our hands. Our true course ought to be, not to interfere in their internal concerns, but to cultivate friendly relations with them, and to endeavour to convince them, by our forbearance and kindly conduct, that their wisest plan is to be on good terms with us, in order that they may derive those advantages from intercourse with us which are sure to follow from the interchange of commodities and mutual benefits.

In all our dealings with these border-tribes we should bear in mind that, though nominally independent, practically they are not so, but are merely representatives of a greater people behind—that is, of Afghanistan. The shadow of our power, indeed, fells far away into Central Asia; consequently, our frontier policy is no mere local matter. We may affect a cold neutrality, but it is not believed in, nor in reality is it possible, and every time we enter the mountains, to burn the villages, destroy the crops, and drive off the cattle, we may rely on it that we sow the seeds of bitter animosities, which only require opportunity to betray themselves.

A study of the map will show us that the physical features of the country almost of themselves indicate the course which our policy should assume. The great range of the Hindoo Koosh, which runs from east to west, lies not far beyond our Indian dominions, and is the real barrier between us and Central Asia, whilst all the mountains of which we have been speaking are but the southerly spurs of this great natural wall of eternal snow; so that the people of Bonair, Swat, Bajour, &c, and even of Afghanistan itself, are as it were our natural allies, and are in possession of our true line of defence. To attempt to advance and rectify our present frontiers by conquest would merely lead to an interminable and exhausting war in an inhospitable region; whereas, by a dexterous and consistent policy, we might not only gain all the benefits of a strong boundary, but brave defenders of it at the same time.

The experience gained in the last Persian war, in 1856–7, tends to prove that this is no fanciful idea. At that time the *Shah* of Persia was in possession of Herat; and being anxious to drive him out, we entered into an agreement with Dost Mahomed, the then ruler of Afghanistan, and subsidised him to the amount of 10,000*l*. sterling a month, so long as the war lasted, and gave him also many thousand stand of arms, and thus accomplished our object. If the simple expedient of a temporary subsidy, to a ruler whose previous experience can hardly have led him to regard us with friendship, were sufficient to purchase his active support at a critical time, may we not feel sanguine that, by a consistent course of conciliation, we should achieve results of a far more satisfactory kind than by the endless expeditions which are now necessary to maintain even a moderate tranquillity on our border?

Glancing still farther north on the map of Asia, it is impossible not to perceive the steady and rapid advance of Russia. Her steamers are on the Caspian and Aral—her fortified posts have been for some time established along the Syr Daria (Jaxartes). We now hear of the conquest of Kokan and of battles in Bokhara, the apparently inevitable result of which will be the adoption of the line of the Oxus. Afghanistan alone will then stand between us and Russia in Central Asia. Now Afghanistan at this moment is in a complete state of anarchy. Dost Mahomed died in 1863, since which time his sons have been fighting over their father's patrimony; and whilst we have resumed our normal attitude of cold indifference, Russian envoys are in the camps of both brothers. It may be, as often asserted, that the vicinity of a great empire will be more advantageous to us in many ways then the dubious friendship of wild Asiatic hordes; but at all events, in that case, the changed circumstances will involve the necessity of a secure frontier.

LEONAUR

ALSO FROM LEONAUR

AVAILABLE IN SOFTCOVER OR HARDCOVER WITH DUST JACKET

AN APACHE CAMPAIGN IN THE SIERRA MADRE *by John G. Bourke*—An Account of the Expedition in Pursuit of the Chiricahua Apaches in Arizona, 1883.

BILLY DIXON & ADOBE WALLS *by Billy Dixon and Edward Campbell Little*—Scout, Plainsman & Buffalo Hunter, *Life and Adventures of "Billy" Dixon* by Billy Dixon and *The Battle of Adobe Walls* by Edward Campbell Little (*Pearson's Magazine*).

WITH THE CALIFORNIA COLUMN *by George H. Petis*—Against Confederates and Hostile Indians During the American Civil War on the South Western Frontier, *The California Column, Frontier Service During the Rebellion* and *Kit Carson's Fight With the Comanche and Kiowa Indians.*

THRILLING DAYS IN ARMY LIFE *by George Alexander Forsyth*—Experiences of the Beecher's Island Battle 1868, the Apache Campaign of 1882, and the American Civil War.

TIGERS ALONG THE TIGRIS *by E. J. Thompson*—The Leicestershire Regiment in Mesopotamia During the First World War.

THE NEZ PERCÉ CAMPAIGN, 1877 *by G. O. Shields & Edmond Stephen Meany*—Two Accounts of Chief Joseph and the Defeat of the Nez Percé, *The Battle of Big Hole* by G. O. Shields and *Chief Joseph, the Nez Percé* by Edmond Stephen Meany.

THE LEAN, BROWN MEN *by Angus Buchanan*—Experiences in East Africa During the Great War with the 25th Royal Fusiliers—the Legion of Frontiersmen..

SHERIDAN'S TROOPERS ON THE BORDERS *by De Benneville Randolph Keim*—The Winter Campaign of the U. S. Army Against the Indian Tribes of the Southern Plains, 1868-9.

LADY SALE'S AFGHANISTAN *by Florentia Sale*—An Indomitable Victorian Lady's Account of the Retreat from Kabul During the First Afghan War.

WILD LIFE IN THE FAR WEST *by James Hobbs*—The Adventures of a Hunter, Trapper, Guide, Prospector and Soldier.

THE FIRST AFGHAN WAR *by Mowbray Morris*—A Brief Sketch 1839-1842.

LIFE IN THE FAR WEST *by George F. Ruxton*—The Experiences of a British Officer in America and Mexico During the 1840's.

ADVENTURES IN MEXICO AND THE ROCKY MOUNTAINS *by George F. Ruxton*—Experiences of Mexico and the South West During the 1840's.

Lightning Source UK Ltd.
Milton Keynes UK
UKOW03f2357140414

229984UK00001B/228/P